GERALDINE FERRARO MAKES HISTORY

THE INITIAL EXCITEMENT

"The reaction has been so extraordinary that you have to wonder: why was there any question about it in the first place? People are excited about politics for the first time this year."

> —*Alice Travis, Democratic head of the National Women's Political Caucus*

"The professional politicians, the men, are ga-ga. The Ferraro selection has unleashed a bigger reservoir of energy and spirit than anyone guessed."

> —*Murray Seeger,*
> *Chief spokesman for the AFL-CIO*

"The first thing I thought of was not winning in the political sense, but of my two daughters. To think of the numbers of young women who can now aspire to anything."

> —*Ann Richards,*
> *State Treasurer of Texas*

GERALDINE

"She's Archie Bunker, she's a religious woman in the Bible Belt, s̶ ̶ ̶ ̶ ̶ ̶ ̶ ̶ ̶ ̶ ̶ ̶ talks plain about kids, s̶ ̶ ̶ ̶ ̶ ̶ ̶ ̶ ̶ ̶ ̶rked hard to get where ̶ ̶ ̶ ̶ ̶ ̶ ̶ ̶ ̶ ̶ ̶ough."

> *̶my Knight,*
> *̶abama chairman*

"She's no cream puff; she's a tough dame."

—*Betty Friedan*

"She adds excitement. She has that star quality."

—*Representative Tony Coelho,*
California

THE FUTURE

"Any time competent and able women are recognized and become visible, a sense of expectation and prowess is engendered among younger women that they too can aspire to new heights."

—*Matina Horner,*
President of Radcliffe College

"A significant advance for women in American politics."

—*Gary Hart*

"Just to have a woman in a key position is very meaningful to all of us."

—*Anne Rudin,*
Mayor of Sacramento

"This impels the electorate and the media to take women's candidacies seriously at all levels. There will be no more jokes."

—*Ruth Mandel,*
Director of Rutgers University's
Center for the American Woman and Politics

"More women are going to be running now and not just licking envelopes."

—*Jody Newman,*
Director of the Women's Campaign Fund

GERRY!

A Woman Making History

Rosemary Breslin
and Joshua Hammer

Introduction by
Gloria Steinem

PINNACLE BOOKS **NEW YORK**

Sources for this book include: Personal interviews, the *National Journal*, *Congressional Quarterly*, *The Washington Post*, *The New York Times*, *Time*, *Newsweek*, *Ms.*, *New York Magazine*, and *People*.

GERRY!

An original Pinnacle Books edition, published for the first time anywhere.

First printing/September 1984

ISBN: 0-523-42444-2
Can. ISBN: 0-523-43424-3

Cover photo by Cynthia Johnson/Time Magazine

Printed in the United States of America

PINNACLE BOOKS, INC.
1430 Broadway
New York, New York 10018

9 8 7 6 5 4 3 2 1

The authors gratefully acknowledge the contribution of the "Women Lawyers" chapter, written by Karen Berger Morello. Karen Berger Morello practices law in New York City and is Historian of the Women's Bar Association of the State of New York. Material contained in this chapter is the result of research for her forthcoming book, *A History of Women Lawyers in the United States,* to be published by Random House.

Special thanks are also extended to: Gloria Steinem, who donated her proceeds to the 1984 Ms. Foundation for Education and Communication, Inc., Phillipa Brophy, Mario Cuomo, Liza Dawson, Gioia Diliberto, Pat Durando, Antonetta Ferraro, Nicholas Ferraro, Timothy Flaherty, Sarah Graves, Michelle Green, Melvin Lebetkin, Sterling Lord, Bill Plummer, John Saar, Frank Silverstein, Frank Smith, Mildred Snyder, Lisa Stockman, and all the other people involved in this project.

CONTENTS

INTRODUCTION

It was four A.M. when a television producer travelling with Mondale's campaign called to tell me that the vice-presidential choice was Ferraro.

"You're kidding," I said, sure that sleep was deceiving me.

"It's official, it's announced," she said, and then, dropping all pretense of journalistic calm, "Isn't it great?"

Three hours later, Bella Abzug and I were on "CBS News" being asked about our reactions. I admitted I had been convinced that a woman wouldn't be chosen. From travelling two or three days a week as a lecturer and feminist organizer, as well as from a Louis Harris/ *Ms.* magazine poll that showed about 70 percent of women and men to favor a woman Vice President in 1984, I knew that most of the public was ready. What

I didn't believe was the readiness of the politicians. Historically, the vice-presidency had been used to imitate the adversary; a tactic that seemed to me outdated, since it tended to disillusion the ticket's natural constituency and reduce its turnout. Nonetheless, that was the conventional wisdom, and I had assumed Mondale would choose someone a few more inches toward Reagan. On the other hand, Bella, who has been the first to predict every political explosion from Vietnam's importance to Nixon's resignation, had been sure all along that a woman, and a pro-equality woman, would be chosen.

It was she who had called meetings of national women leaders and key Democratic Congresswomen two years before to discuss the possible pledging of convention delegates, regardless of their presidential choice, to a particular woman Vice President. The plan had foundered on the inability of Congresswomen to risk their political seriousness by making such a move at the time. Nonetheless, the idea had caught fire on its own. After all the Democratic candidates had promised to seriously consider a woman, a Jesse Jackson had brought the idea to a wider audience by pledging to choose a woman, the vice-presidency had become the focus of questions put to Mondale wherever he went.

"It wasn't pressure," Bella explained, "after all, major political women and organizations had endorsed Mondale, whether or not he chose a woman. The fact is that it's smart politics—and it's a tribute to Mondale that he recognized it. Ferraro will bring the enthusiasm factor, and an increased turnout from exactly the groups he needs to win."

Even so, neither of us was prepared for the depth of emotion this choice would elicit.

By the accident of being a recognizable part of this change, I'm treated to reactions every day: in the street, from saleswomen, from cab drivers, from women and men who themselves didn't guess the impact of seeing a woman, and a pro-equality woman like Ferraro, honored in authority.

Yes, Ferraro is being questioned and scrutinized with an intensity not directed at male Vice Presidents. The double standard is not dead. As a member of Congress, she had had more foreign policy experience than Reagan or Carter had as governors. In number of years in Congress, she has had as much experience as Nixon did when he was chosen by Eisenhower. As a woman, she has been praised for spending time in supermarkets, assessed for her clothes and hair, or questioned about etiquette in a way her male counterpart would not.

But the sight of a woman in a position of potential national leadership and trust may have more longterm importance than we can guess in this election year.

Up to now, female authority has been experienced by women and men mostly in the home and in childhood. That has made many of us mistrust women as authority figures outside the home: to accept their power seemed a dangerous regression; a flight from the rationality and wisdom of the male power we associate with adulthood and the public world; or even a fear that women in power would have to become like men. It's a division that has penalized all of us: men, by assuming that they can't be emotional and nurturing; women, by assuming they can't be rational and achieving; the country, by suppressing half its human talent.

In the long run, the importance of the Ferraro factor may be the talent and dreams it unleashes in others.

In the short run, the energy is visible every day. As a homemaker *and* a professional woman, she allows almost every woman to hook into some part of her experience. As a symbolic break in the three major ways we have selected our leadership, by sex, by ethnic group, and by class, she raises hopes that go far beyond her own role.

On a sunny New York street not long after Ferraro's nomination, a jogger passed me.

"Isn't it great!" this black man in his thirties shouted. "Now *you* can be President."

"No, *you* can be President," I yelled back.

He grinned. "Now we *all* could be President," he said.

And that's true.

—Gloria Steinem
July 27, 1984

PROLOGUE

"Ladies and gentlemen of the convention, my name is Geraldine Ferraro. I stand before you to proclaim tonight: America is a land where dreams can come true for all of us. . . . Tonight the daughter of an immigrant from Italy has been chosen to run for President in the new land my father came to love."

The improbable event, the untested step, the announcement that released a surge of excitement and trepidation among men and women across America, had happened at last. For two weeks the country had watched as Walter Mondale interviewed a rainbow lineup of vice-presidential contenders, from the Jewish woman Mayor of San Francisco to the Hispanic Mayor of San Antonio to the Black Mayor of Los Angeles to the Congresswoman from Queens. It was a process trumpeted by some as demonstrating the Democrats' broad appeal and the tremendous societal progress made since the 1960s. Others lampooned it as a desperate attempt at minority appeasement. But when Geraldine Ferraro stood before the Democratic National Convention at San Francisco's Moscone Center on Thursday night, July 19, 1984, all the skepticism, all the charges of tokenism, seemed to vanish in the magic of the moment. Never before had a woman received such a vote of national confidence; never before had she stood so close—"an election away from a heartbeat away," as *Time* put it—to the most powerful office on earth.

> "As I stand before the American people and think of the great honor this convention has bestowed upon me, I recall the words of Dr. Martin Luther King, Jr., who made America stronger by making America more free. He said: 'Occasionally in life there are moments which cannot be completely explained by words. Their meaning can only be articulated by the inaudible language of the heart.' Tonight is such a moment for me. My heart is filled with pride."

It is worth looking back for a moment to gain some perspective on how attitudes have changed in a few short decades toward the prospect of a woman in high office. In 1934 Eleanor Roosevelt tossed the idea aside, saying simply, "I don't think we've reached that point." In 1937, only a third of all Americans said they would consider voting a woman for President, according to a Gallup poll. Fifteen years later, Margaret Chase Smith (Republican of Maine), who served four terms in the United States Senate and was the first woman to have her name put in nomination as the presidential candidate of a major party, was asked what she would do if she woke up one day in the White House. "I'd go straight to Mrs. Truman and apologize," she replied, "then I'd go home." The prospect of a female Chief Executive still seemed so ludicrous in 1964 that Hollywood lampooned it in the slapstick comedy *Kisses for My President*, in which politico Polly Bergen gets elected, then has to resign when hubby Fred MacMurray gets her pregnant. Back in 1970, the noted surgeon Edgar Berman suggested that women were simply too emotional for positions of high power because of their hormonal chemistry. But by then the public mood was changing. In 1969, 50 percent of Americans surveyed by Gallup said they would consider voting for a female presidential candidate; by last year, the number had risen to 80 percent.

And now it had happened. History had been made. "There's an electricity in the air, an excitement, a sense of new possibilities and of pride," declared Geraldine Ferraro shortly after she was named as Mondale's choice. And virtually nobody—neither friend nor foe —could disagree with her. The selection, said Chief Justice G. Mennen Williams of the Michigan State Supreme Court, "is at the cutting edge of history. Sexual equality is overdue by a generation. Changes like this have given courage to the fainthearted to do what they wanted to do anyway and have convinced those not favorably disposed that failure to progress will no longer be tolerated." Feminists rejoiced at their greatest triumph since the achievement of universal suffrage sixty-four years ago. "All our lives we have been empowering other people, our children, our husbands, our families. This week we have the power," said Ann Smith, an adviser to Gary Hart's campaign, at the convention. "I didn't know how deeply I would feel about it," said Gloria Steinem. "It has brought out so many hopes and dreams." Bella Abzug, at a dinner with a group of women a week before the convention, pulled out a cigar from her purse, twirled it, and proclaimed, "It's a girl!" Even President Reagan, while disparaging Ferraro's criticism of his programs and her charge that he was not "a good Christian," called her nomination "a logical step and one that possibly is overdue." But perhaps Congresswoman Mary Rose Oakar of Ohio said it best, after addressing a seminar of working women at a junior college in Cleveland shortly after Mondale's announcement. "The excitement and the enthusiasm that we all had for each other in that room was electrifying," she said. "Here we were trying to talk about how women can attain policy-making goals, whether in office or small business or a hospital, and after Mondale's announcement, we knew we could do anything."

But after all the celebration, after the talk of Ferraro as a "living symbol of change," after the satisfaction of seeing sixty years of progress well up into an ineffable moment of triumph, after speculation on the vistas to come, there were serious questions to consider. What would the Ferraro selection mean for the

4

Democratic Party's chances in November? Would the daring choice galvanize enough Democratic voters—in particular, female voters—to defeat the Teflon-coated Ronald Reagan? How would the choice of a liberal, Queens, three-term Congresswoman go over in the conservative South, a must-win region for the Democrats? "The idea of that new ingredient, the mysterious factor of the female vote, makes Ferraro a high-risk, high-gain pick," asserted Democratic Governor Richard Lamm of Colorado. Both Republicans and Democrats agreed that Mondale's very gamble has roused new interest in what might otherwise have been a ho-hum campaign. Republican Chairman Howard ("Bo") Callaway, former campaign manager for Gerald Ford, called the Ferraro choice "the first excitement, the first nonmush I've seen in Mondale's political career." Peter Kelley, the California Democratic Chairman, said, "There was a sense of invincibility about Ronald Reagan coming into this convention among many Democrats, but I think the nomination of Mrs. Ferraro changes that. Now there's optimism and hope that this ticket can win." Added Senator Christopher Dodd of Connecticut, "There's no question the ticket is behind, but it's certainly within reaching distance, whereas before we got here there was concern that this was a lost cause. Now there's new life breathed into this campaign. Democrats are feeling good about it."

Whether this new breath of life can bring in the numbers is another question. In Ferraro's favor, pundits point out that her background and ideology can snare a broad range of constituencies. She is a first-generation Italian-American, a liberal Congresswoman from the blue-collar "Archie Bunker" district, a religious Catholic who personally opposes abortion but remains prochoice, an upwardly mobile career woman with a close-knit family, and a firm believer in "a strong, sensible defense" who "wants nothing to do with reckless adventures in Latin America." It is a combination that can strike a chord with Yuppies and urban ethnics, hawks and doves, conservatives and liberals alike. "She unites the ticket," says James Quackenbush, the campaign's southern coordinator. He expects Ferraro to perform well in his region, which has lagged behind the rest of the nation in its acceptance of female politicians, and Jimmy Knight, the Alabama campaign chairman, shares his confidence. "She's Archie Bunker, she's a religious woman in the Bible Belt, she's a mother and gets down and talks plain about kids, she's a wife and supportive, she's worked hard to get where she is...she's tough," he said. "You betcha she'll sell in Alabama."

Democratic campaign strategists are also, naturally, focusing their hopes on Ferraro's ability to seize the "gender-gap" issue and turn it to the Democrats' advantage. Believing that a large turnout from female voters could close the 8.4-million-vote margin of Reagan's 1980 victory, Democrats in thirty-two states have begun forming teams to bring out the more than thirty-three million women who remain unregistered (about seven million new women voters have already registered). The Women's Vote Project, a coalition of sixty-eight women's organizations in twenty states, is working in day-care centers, bowling alleys, K Mart stores, college campuses, and food-stamp centers to register low-income women; the Human Service Fund has established a goal to add five million new low-income voters to the rolls by election day. Also involved are such groups as the National Coalition of Black Voter Participation, the National Puerto Rico/Hispanic Participation Project, and the League of Women Voters Education Fund. Whether they will come anywhere near their ambitious goals is impossible to predict, as is the power Ferraro has to galvanize already-registered female voters.

Even if Ferraro does exploit the gender gap successfully and rally women around her, the Democrats face serious problems. Peter Hart, Walter Mondale's pollster, believes that for the party to succeed, it will need to pull in 85 percent of Democratic voters this year; up until the convention, polls were showing that only 70 percent were willing to stick with the party in 1984. And President Reagan remains a formidable opponent; with a soaring popularity rating, a strong economy, and ample "photo opportunities," he is clearly in the driver's seat.

But the Democratic strategy is to exploit what they believe is Reagan's weakness and their strength: the vision each offers of the future. They will portray the President as a leader forcing his country to live on borrowed money and borrowed time. "If we can get across that this is a false economy, I think that'll give us a shot at it," says Charles Whitehead, the Florida party chairman. And they will continue to present Ferraro as they have been doing during and since the convention: as a dynamic choice who opens up a world

7

of possibility—for women, for minorities, for youth, for anyone who believes, as Ferraro expressed it, that "in America, anything is possible if you work for it."

"When we speak of the future," said Walter Mondale, accepting the Democratic Party's 1984 presidential nomination, "we speak of Gerry Ferraro." And even if the Mondale-Ferraro ticket goes down in defeat this November, virtually everybody seemed to agree: the future did, indeed, belong to Gerry.

1

THE EARLY YEARS

The story began on a Sunday afternoon in May of 1926, not far from where it ended more than a half century later, in Queens. Antonetta Corrieri and her parents were visiting a friend on Thirty-sixth Street in Astoria. Dominick Ferraro, who had emigrated to Queens from the small Italian town of Marcianise, was waiting outside the house with some friends. He was on his way to an Italian feast.

"Come on inside," Dominick's cousin Carl said. Carl wanted to introduce him to Antonetta Corrieri. Antonetta was from Manhattan where her parents worked as a street cleaner and a dressmaker.

Once inside, Carl noticed that Dominick didn't take his eyes off the twenty-one-year-old girl.

"He's looking at you," Carl said.

"He doesn't even know me," the girl answered.

But just a few minutes later, Dominick asked Carl if he thought Antonetta would go out with him. Carl told him she was pretty fussy but to give it a try.

With the feast forgotten, Dominick offered Mr. Corrieri and his wife a ride home to Manhattan. He asked Antonetta for a date, but she said no. "My mother was strict," she recalled. "She wouldn't have let me. But he was in love with me the first time he met me."

Her mother finally did allow her daughter to go on a few dates with him, but "I had to bring my niece along," Antonetta said. "Finally I said I'm old enough. If I can't go alone, I won't go at all."

Since Mrs. Corrieri had told her daughter on more than one occasion that she wanted Antonetta married before she died, the mother gave in.

Two months later Dominick presented Antonetta with a ring. They got married in October. "That's it," Mrs. Ferraro said. "And we courted while we were married. For the entire seventeen years."

In Newburgh, a quiet river city sixty miles north of New York, Dominick Ferraro opened the Roxy Restaurant on the corner of Mill and West Parmenter streets. In the back of the restaurant was a garden, and the family lived on the floor above. But back in the early 1930s, it was a place where a man from Marcianise, Italy, and his young wife tried to make a future for themselves.

They soon had children. Antonetta's first two were twins, Carl and Anthony, but Anthony died after three days. Her third son, Gerard, was killed in an automobile accident at the age of three. Two years later Geraldine was born.

In the meat market on Mill Street, just up the block from the Ferraro's old building, seventy-three-year-old Frank Eanni recalled his friend Dominick Ferraro. "We've been in this spot since nineteen thirty-three," Mr. Eanni said. "Dominick used to call me to deliver meat to the restaurant. Dominick was a tall, handsome man with black, wavy hair. Even though business was tough back then, he was always a happy-go-lucky and friendly man. We used to talk. But even then, I think he had a little high blood pressure." When business in the restaurant grew too slow, Mr. Ferraro converted the restaurant into the Mill Street Five and Ten.

Although Antonetta Ferraro's main job was raising her children, nobody, including Mr. Eanni, remembers her as just a housewife. "She was quite a worker," he said. "One of the old-timers."

Beulah Politi's kitchen window faced the Ferraro's house. She remembers Dominick Ferraro as a quiet man and Antonetta Ferraro as a woman who "sweat herself off to see that good things came for her children. Her children were her whole life."

While the family struggled to make a living, more adversity struck. In 1933, with three-year-old Gerard asleep in her arms, the family was involved in a car accident. Gerard died, and a critically injured Antonetta demanded that all her son's toys be buried with him.

For the next two years Antonetta stopped going to church at Sacred Heart and continuously washed and pressed her dead son's clothes. The family doctor finally recommended that Mrs. Ferraro try to get over the boy's death by having another child.

11

Geraldine Anne Ferraro was born August 26, 1935, in her parents' home. "I was afraid to go to the hospital because they would put me to sleep," Mrs. Ferraro said. "So they soaked the sheets in Lysol and water and put the instruments on the stove. I didn't let my husband in the bedroom. But when it was over he was allowed to come in." When Mr. Ferraro looked at the hefty ten-and-a-half pound girl in the crib, he said to his wife, "She's grown already."

Geraldine was immediately the focus of her father's devotion. Antonetta Ferraro remembers that he bought Geraldine a new dress each month, constantly brought her little toys, and always called her "princess." Geraldine remembers that she was given everything because her father felt that Gerard had been brought back to life. By eleven months Geraldine weighed thirty pounds and had taken her first steps, which were, like her brothers' before her, inside the playpen. Her mother felt the floor was too dirty. "All my children learned to walk on a pad in the playpen."

"I used to go over and stay for an hour to watch her," Mrs. Politi said. "Her mother kept her like a little doll. I can still picture her little curls."

When Geraldine was two, the family moved to number 50 Dubois Street, a three-story brick house with a turret. "It was such a beautiful house," Mrs. Ferraro remembers. "Anybody who came to my house then has good memories of it." In that house, Geraldine and Helen Farina played and told secrets. "I don't remember not knowing her," said Helen Farina Angelo, whose cousins had lived across the street from the Ferraros on Mill Street. "Geraldine and I were

12

really like sisters. When you saw one, you saw two," Mrs. Angelo said. The two girls did what other little girls still do. "Paper dolls were really big. Jump rope. Hopscotch. Now when people ask me if she was political, I laugh. We played mother, teacher, and nurse." Mrs. Angelo remembered that their mothers dressed them alike and that they wore their hair in banana curls.

The two girls both attended Casa San Jose school, a private Catholic school on the Mount St. Mary grounds. Even before Gerry was old enough to start school, her mother had taught her at home, just as Geraldine Ferraro later did with her own daughter.

Mrs. Ferraro remembers that even in those early years her daughter was always a good listener. "When I'd be sitting around in the kitchen drinking coffee and having cake, she would never interrupt. And whenever someone came in, she'd get up from her chair and move even though there were lots of other chairs around the table. She knew enough to respect her elders."

Then, when Geraldine was eight, her father complained of chest pains. The next day, at the age of forty-four, he had a heart attack and died. "When she woke up the next morning, she asked, 'Why is Daddy so still?' and I told her that he had gone to heaven."

After her husband's death, Mrs. Ferraro moved from Newburgh to Longfellow Avenue in the Bronx so she could be closer to her relatives. She never returned to Newburgh. "I let everything die when my husband died. I lost a son in Newburgh and a husband. It wasn't Newburgh's fault, but what would I go back for?"

"Until her father died, all Geraldine thought about was what things to play with," Mrs. Ferraro recalled.

"Then her world turned upside down. Carl would cry. But Gerry didn't. She was like me." And, like her mother, the daughter hid her grief. Gerry was left behind to board at Mount St. Mary's for a brief time. She recently told an interviewer, "Oh, how I missed my mother so . . . and my father gone. I would hear the train go by and the whistle . . . and I would cry myself to sleep. . . . You know, it's just a void that you grow up with. I look at my daughters with their father, and I can't tell you what it does to me. I so love to see my son with his father when he comes home. To me, that is the most wonderful thing."

Mrs. Ferraro wasn't happy in the six-room apartment on Longfellow Avenue. "It was my sister's idea, not mine. She wanted me to be close by so she could be with me," said Mrs. Ferraro. "Even then it wasn't such a hot neighborhood."

Mrs. Ferraro then put Geraldine into Marymount School in Tarrytown, where she was again a boarder and for a time considered becoming a nun. Gerry was a member of the honor society, the debating club, the French club, and the literary society. She also played field hockey, basketball, softball, and swam.

Both Mrs. Ferraro and Gerry had a difficult time adjusting to the downhill turn the family's finances had taken. "When my daughter came down from school, she didn't like the apartment. She was used to a beautiful house.

"I never said to my children. 'Your father's dead. You've got to go to work,'" said Mrs. Ferraro, who supported her family by crocheting beads on wedding dresses and evening gowns so she could afford to send Geraldine and Carl to parochial school. "I did say, 'If you don't work hard, you'll get nowhere.'"

When Geraldine asked her mother to teach her bead-work, she responded that it would be better if she stuck to her education. Geraldine Ferraro recalled this in a 1982 commencement address. "When I was about fourteen or fifteen, I asked my mother to teach me her skill. She was a crochet beader. She sat me down at the frame, put a needle in my hand, and showed me how to attack bead after bead. For about ten minutes, my mother watched patiently as I attached about ten beads. Finally, she took the needle out of my hand and said, 'Gerry, you'd better go to college or you'll starve to death.'"

Her mother says Gerry was actually quite adept at sewing the beads. "She learned quick, but I didn't want her to learn. I left school after eighth grade and wanted an education so bad I could taste it. So I said if I have to scrub floors, my children are going to have what I never did have—an education."

During those very lean years, Mrs. Ferraro never mentioned her husband. "I always felt it, but their loss was so great that I tried to keep from reminding them. I never cried in front of my children, but my pillow knows."

Once she could afford it, Mrs. Ferraro moved the family out of the Bronx and back to Queens—into a two-bedroom $65-a-month apartment in Astoria.

Geraldine was already moving at the fast pace that later marked her career. With the attitude that there

15

was no time to waste, she skipped the seventh and eighth grades and graduated from Marymount High School in 1952 at the age of sixteen.

It was then that her mother bought her the $70 ivory silk with lace Lord & Taylor graduation dress that, if it still existed, might have someday been placed in the Smithsonian. Antonetta Ferraro, determined that her daughter would be dressed as well as the rich kids in the class, scrimped and saved and lived without meat for months in order to buy her daughter the dress, the same dress that Patsy Bush, a rich kid in the class, wore. Her mother had proved that, despite all that had happened, they were a family of survivors who looked ahead, not behind.

Addressing an Order of the Sons of Italy lodge in 1981, Geraldine Ferraro recalled that "when my mother's brothers and sisters tried to talk her out of sending me to college, she responded: *'Se si educa un uomo, si educa l'uomo solo, se si educa una donna, si educa tutta una famiglia.'* Which means, of course, when you educate a man, you educate only a man, but when you educate a woman, you educate an entire family."

Geraldine continued on and received a full scholarship to Marymount Manhattan College. She worked her way through school by selling handkerchiefs at Bloomingdale's and also took teacher education courses at Hunter College. She earned a bachelor of arts degree in 1956.

"While we were knitting argyle socks in college, Gerry was knitting argyle sweaters," recalled Nancy Keating, a good friend.

Geraldine Ferraro had a brief and unsatisfying job

as a legal secretary before becoming a schoolteacher. She had wanted to become a doctor but became a teacher instead, "because women did not become doctors in the fifties," she said. While she taught second grade at P.S. 85 in Astoria, she used to stop in at her cousin Nick Ferraro's office. "She liked teaching," he recalled, "but it wasn't enough for her. She has such drive. If she hadn't gone into public life, I think she would have just kept getting degrees. Law school. Medical school and on and on."

Geraldine Ferraro put herself through Fordham Law School at night by teaching elementary school in Queens during the day. After a day spent with children, she spent her evening with men who weren't overenthusiastic about her being there; she was one of two women in a class of 179. With determination she went about the task of obtaining her law degree.

"You really can't imagine a greater contrast between a woman's job and a man's," she once told an upstate New York audience. "After a day of second graders, off I would go to Fordham University to sit in a law class with just one other woman and a string of male professors who sincerely believed I was taking a man's rightful place."

Although she graduated with honors, it didn't mean very much to the men on Wall Street. "In nineteen sixty, five job interviews at one of our prestigious New York law firms culminated with a 'you're terrific, but we're not hiring any women this year,'" she said. She was admitted to the New York State Bar in March 1961.

Just a few days after graduating from law school,

she married John A. Zaccaro. She had been friends with him for almost five years, having been introduced to him by Nancy Keating. "We both come from Italian families, and we talked about what I was going to do, and he said, 'Why?' And he said, 'My mother never worked.' And I said, 'She's your mother and I love her, but she's not a lawyer.'"

2

THE QUEENS HOUSEWIFE

The early years of the Zaccaros' marriage had its share of struggling-young-couple stories. Her husband remembers himself as a failure in his father's real estate business. "I had a lot of hard knocks," he said. "Everything went wrong." Too proud to ask his father for an advance, he struggled. John Zaccaro remembers walking in the snow to the movies with his pregnant wife and then taking a cab home. The fare was less than a dollar. Mr. Zaccaro handed the driver the $1 bill, turned, and walked into the house. Once inside, he realized he had mistakenly given away a $10 bill. "I was sick," he said.

But things improved when he began buying commercial property in Soho, Greenwich Village, and Chinatown.

Although Geraldine Ferraro worked part time as a

lawyer in her husband's office, most of the 1960s and early 1970s were spent as a housewife in Forest Hills Gardens and raising the three children she had in four years: Donna, now twenty-two, John, now twenty, and Laura, eighteen.

In Forest Hills she was known as Mrs. Zaccaro to the friends of her children and Gerry to the adults. Her children attended the nursery school at the Community House on Borage Place, and many of the women who live in her neighborhood met her while they waited to pick up their children from school.

Arlene D'Arienzo recalled standing outside the nursery school on a winter's day in 1967, waiting for her daughter Carmel and Donna Zaccaro to be let out. "What do you want to be when you grow up?" she asked her friend Geraldine. The two women giggled because, in Queens as in most of the world, if you were married and had children and could afford not to work, you didn't. Maybe when the kids grew up, you could go back to school, dabble in law, or get a real estate license, but that was many years away and, hopefully, by then you'd have mellowed and decided that you were fortunate enough just to live in a large house in an elegant enclave where the trappings of success were great and the pressures from the world outside were few. Perhaps Geraldine Ferraro's greatest test during these years was for her not to allow the days to turn into years and then into a lifetime among the flagstones and turrets and gables.

Forest Hills Gardens is a 175-acre incorporated community with 865 homes. It was developed seventy-six years ago as the first planned community in the country. The streets of this neighborhood are quiet and filled with strong, old maples, benches in parks, and cherry-blossom trees that bloom in May and dogwoods shortly after. It is a neighborhood of winding streets where the residents' cars have identifying stickers on them and signs along the way say Privately Owned Streets and No Parking Anytime. When Tip O'Neill came to visit her home, he bellowed, "I thought you told me you lived in Queens."

Inside these gates the main worries of a mother are what school the children should be sent to, where to vacation in winter, and where to pass the days of summer. In the fall the routine starts all over again. The most serious conversations are about how to stop people from picking the flowers in front of the houses and how to keep the teenagers from taking over the parks at night and from racing about the streets in their parents' cars.

Mrs. Zaccaro and her family played tennis at the elite West Side Tennis Club, with its green ivy and small sign outside that says Members Only.

She and her husband shopped at Gristede's on Austin Street where, according to Mrs. Zaccaro, she comparison shopped and used coupons. "She was just like the rest of the mothers," said Mrs. Massie, another neighbor.

And every Sunday morning, the Zaccaro family attended mass at Our Lady of Mercy Roman Catholic Church on Kessel Street. "The thing I most remember about them was how put together they were. We'd roll out of bed and go to church and there the Zaccaros would be, looking like the perfect family," said Carmel D'Arienzo.

Mrs. Zaccaro threw birthday parties for her children, took them to swimming class on Saturday morning, and taught swimming at the Community House. She attended every family function and sat down to a family dinner each night; she had a full-time housekeeper to help. She and her husband joined the Maggios to chase kids away from the gulley across the street where they drank beer and left the cans behind. She proved she could be calm in a crisis when a neighbor's car rolled backward down the hill and wrecked her new station wagon and well-tended bushes. She simply walked up the block, rang the bell, and said, "Do you own a green Volvo?" When the answer was affirmative, she continued, "Well, it's wrecked our new car and it's now in the hedges."

"She was a regular mother, you know," her twenty-two-year-old daughter, Donna, said. "She was always shuttling me from lesson to lesson. Everything under the sun. Swimming. Piano. Dancing. Asking, 'Why didn't you get an A?'"

About Geraldine Ferraro's hard youth, her daughter Donna said, "My mother didn't talk about it a lot. Sure, every so often she'd hit us with, 'You have it so much easier than I did,' but that was really it." Before Donna was old enough to go to school, her mother taught her to read and write so well that Donna only went to P.S. 101 for a few days. Since her mother didn't want her to skip grades the way she had, Donna was sent to Marymount.

In the early years, the children were sent to Sacred Heart, Marymount, and St. David's, which were the correct schools for the children of this insulated neighborhood. Each weekday morning, at 7:20, Mr. Zaccaro would load his own kids and a slew of others into the station wagon and shuttle them off to Manhattan.

When school was let out for vacations, the family went to Acapulco, Antigua, and Barbados, and during the summer they went to Salt Air on Fire Island.

Her house was well ordered and her children well-behaved. In 1982 she described her life at this time: "In November of nineteen seventy-three, I and my husband were a successful middle-class couple. We were financially secure, having gone to graduate schools and achieved a measure of success in our community. We had three children, two homes, a dog, belonged to the right clubs, and played pretty good tennis. That year, when we went to vote, there were numerous referenda on the ballot . . . all costing money. We came out of the polling place and compared notes, and I said to my husband, 'I guess you can call us conservatives.' We had made it on our own and were not about to have our hard-earned tax dollars go to the do-nothings of society. We had worked hard to get where we were and so could they."

"We always said if you saw the way she ran a kitchen, you knew she could run General Motors," said Pat Durando, who lived around the corner. Another neighbor, Joan Kaufman, recalled the way she tackled cooking. The two women went to an Italian butcher and Gerry ordered a strange-looking piece of meat.

23

"That's horrible," Mrs. Kaufman said. "What is it? Goat or something like that?"

"You'd eat it," Mrs. Zaccaro replied.

"If it comes in a pot, then I eat it. Gerry, how could you cook that thing?"

"If I don't know how to do it," she answered, "no one will ever do it for my children." Even at home Ferraro was always willing to take the extra step.

Mrs. Ferraro told a group of women last year that she was distressed by the Reagan administration's effort to "create the impression that good wives and outstanding mothers are only those who stay at home."

"I don't disparage that," she said. "I did it myself, until the youngest was in second grade. But not every woman can afford to do that."

After thirteen years of being a housewife, Geraldine Ferraro moved out of the kitchen and into the world. As Pat Durando said, "She just took one giant step out of the kitchen."

3

QUEENS POLITICS

The women stood outside the Union Turnpike subway station wrapped in their heavy winter coats. Even in the rain and the snow there were always a few dozen picketers carrying signs that said Stop Lefrak.

In the mornings the women would greet their husbands, who were on their way to work, and later they said hello to their school-bound children.

It was January 1972 and the women of Forest Hills Gardens were trying to stop construction of two twenty-story apartment houses on Union Turnpike. "Twenty-story cliffs" is what the women called the Lefrak organization's buildings, which were already in the initial state of construction.

The women picketed and petitioned, charging that the buildings on the edge of the Gardens would severely strain facilities and ruin the quality of life in the community of private homes and small apartment houses. It was the most vocal political action anyone from staid Forest Hills Gardens had ever seen. It was also Gerry Zaccaro's big political debut.

She didn't handle any of the legal work because many of the husbands were lawyers and they viewed her as a "lightweight," since she wasn't practicing full time. After a debate between two women about whether Gerry could handle a job they had in mind for her, it was decided that she could. She was put in charge of organizing a house tour to help raise money. One of the reasons she was given the job was because her children went to school in Manhattan, so the other women figured she knew how these things could be done with sophistication. And she did. She wrote up short biographies about the houses and acted as hostess during the tours. "She was good at the people things," one woman remembered. Gerry's skills were used to make badges and signs for the meetings held at the local elementary school.

A Queens lawyer, a friend of a friend, was brought in to help their cause. Mario Cuomo had made a name for himself a few years before when he had stopped the demolition of sixty-nine houses in Corona. This was the first time the two had met.

"As a matter of fact, she was just Gerry Zaccaro then," Governor Cuomo said. "She was a housewife, one of the organizers." He remembered her as being "very lively, peppy." He added, "She was a knock-out."

The battle to stop the construction of the buildings ended in the court of appeals, where the opposing group lost. But then the Forest Hills group turned their attentions on the board of directors of the Gardens Corporation, charging that it was their lack of action that had allowed the construction to start in the first place. When it was time for the next election, the group formed an opposing slate, the first time this had ever happened in the history of the Gardens Corporation. Until then it had always been a male-inherited group, with sons taking over when fathers retired. Although the new opposing group was unable to elect any of its candidates to the higher positions, they managed to fill a few of the lower ones. Geraldine Ferraro was elected to the legal committee and put in charge of bylaws.

Even there, she left her mark and showed that she could protect the interests of her constituents. When Granston Tower, a huge house on Greenway North, was sold to Orthodox Jews, word got around the neighborhood that the new owners planned to install a congregation in the house, as the religious Jews had done in many of the homes in nearby Kew Gardens. The neighborhood network of phone calling began and everyone was set for a good fight, but the sale was stopped when Mrs. Ferraro found that the house could only be used as a residence. That alone made her a hero to many members of the community.

Life As A Prosecutor

Gerry first mentioned to her husband and her friends that she was thinking of working for her cousin, Nick Ferraro, the newly appointed Queens District Attorney, at a dinner at the West Side Tennis Club. John Zaccaro, who was unhappy with her decision, said, "I think every woman should have a fourth child."

Still, at Nick Ferraro's victory celebration, Geraldine Ferraro decided to feel her cousin out.

"What's the chances of my becoming an assistant D.A.?" she asked.

"If the screening committee says 'qualified,' then you get the job," he answered.

Nicholas Ferraro, mindful of a political scandal that had preceded him, named a special panel to pass on the qualifications of all assistant district attorneys that were to be hired. Among those on the panel was Mario Cuomo, whose name at the time was an indication that quality and not clubhouse connections was the prime reason for employment in the D.A.'s office.

One of the first applications was from Geraldine Ferraro of 22 Deepdene Road, Forest Hills.

"Her application came back marked 'qualified,'" Nicholas Ferraro recalls. "I was very proud. Mario must have loved seeing another Italian Catholic coming into politics. Particularly a woman. Italian men are famous for wanting women to get ahead."

Nick Ferraro's recent jab at Cuomo's Italian-male status is ironic, given that it was Cuomo's staunch

28

support of Ferraro during his Logan Airport meeting with Walter Mondale that put Geraldine Ferraro onto the ticket.

It was Nick Ferraro who unofficially told Queens that his cousin had been picked by Mondale. On the long Wednesday night when the rumors were circulating, a call was made from the Queens County Democratic Headquarters to Nicholas Ferraro's house. His wife answered and said he wasn't in.

At Democratic headquarters, the man making the call hung up and shouted: "Gerry must have it. Nicky is hiding and he has his wife lying for him. That's Queens right to the end."

But it was January 1974 now, and all that was in the future. Though she had virtually no experience in criminal law, Geraldine Ferraro was appointed assistant district attorney.

(Just two short years before, when interviews were being held for assistant district attorney jobs in Queens, the men went before the screening committee ahead of the women. When all the men were finished being interviewed, someone ducked his head outside, scanned the small group, and said, "Sorry, we've filled all the positions.")

On the vacation the family took in Canada before she started her new job, Gerry took along books on penal law and the code of criminal procedure.

Mrs. Ferraro's first assignment was in the Investigations Bureau, which conducted long-term inquiries and helped prepare cases for trial. She arrived most mornings by 8 A.M., always took files home with her, and was often at work on weekends. "She tried to learn as much as possible as fast as possible," said Timothy Flaherty, a former District Attorney who shared an office with her for two and a half years.

"It was my habit every couple of weeks to take four or five members of the staff to lunch," Nick Ferraro said. "Whenever the hour was up, Gerry would get up to leave. I told her, 'I'm the boss. Take ten extra minutes.' But she said, 'No,' and would leave. When she disagreed with me, she'd come in and argue. She was always very independent. She'll take no quarter and will ask for no quarter."

Although Mrs. Ferraro's bureau usually turned over cases for trial to other prosecutors, she conducted several trials herself, wanting to gain courtroom experience. Frank Smith, a family friend, had been elected to the New York State Supreme Court as a trial judge. "One day in nineteen seventy-four, right after she'd been sworn in, she came to me and said that she wanted to sit in on cases and watch business. Then she started trying cases, and I was the trial judge on many where she was the prosecutor."

In 1975 Mrs. Ferraro moved to the newly created Special Victims Bureau, which was established for charges involving abuse of the elderly and children and for rape cases. John Santucci, who succeeded Nick Ferraro as D.A., made her head of the bureau in 1977.

At the Special Victims Bureau, she immediately became a hero to the children and senior citizens. "Much later I came to the conclusion that she was uniquely successful with children and seniors because they regarded her as a mother figure. She could put them at ease and be supportive of them in a way no man could," Flaherty recalled. The reward for her ability was to hear about incest and beatings and rape. "They were debilitating cases."

"She was very angry at the people who committed these crimes, but she could understand their rage and frustration," Flaherty recalled. "Most were poor, no money, no men in the house, too many men, drunk, drugs. We came in after the fact. It got frustrating not being able to do anything about the problems that caused it," he said.

At night Mrs. Ferraro would lie awake thinking about the cases that filled her day. One case involved a five-year-old girl who had been raped. Ferraro took her testimony while she held the crying child in her lap. "Some of my cases were so horrifying that I can't get the images out of my head. I remember once there was a two-and-a-half-year-old child who had been dipped in boiling water. By the time I got to the case, he was dead—he had locked himself in the refrigerator."

In the case of the scalded boy, the defense lawyer found Mrs. Ferraro to be a difficult opponent who showed no mercy. Judge Smith, her family friend, presided over this particular case. "There were pictures of the child. His skin looked like pieces of mozzarella cheese. Hundreds of long strands of skin. But I was the judge. I stressed there was insufficient evidence. There were no witnesses and the defendant denied the crime. So I ruled there was insufficient evidence."

At dinner the next night, the Zaccaro children told Judge Smith, "We're not talking to you anymore. You made our mother cry." He explained that he hadn't made her cry; frustration had. "That was the case that broke her," Judge Smith said.

Although she showed none of the stress to those who worked with her, even her cousin, Nick Ferraro, fell for her hard front. "When you see the victims of these types of crimes, every human being responds emotionally. You just get past that. She was always very objective."

Her neighbor Pat Durando said, "Gerry saw too much. It became a real burden. It was very hard on her. Extremely hard for her to see the things that people do."

"She'd come home screaming at night and would want to talk shop," remembered neighbor David Blanksteen. "There is nothing worse than a battered woman. Gerry would rail about the injustices of the system and society."

And despite the hard work and dedication she displayed, she was not paid as much as the men who held similar positions in her office. In 1982 she told the National Association of Women Judges: "As a bureau chief in the D.A.'s office many years later, I learned that I was being paid less than men with similar responsibilities. When I asked why, I was told, 'You don't really need the money, Gerry, you've got a husband.'"

She did, however, come away with a better understanding of the circumstances. "I don't like labels," Mr. Flaherty said. "But she came in as a conservative

Democrat and she left with a clearer understanding of all the circumstances involved." She also left "mentally exhausted" and "determined to try to effect a change in the society," according to Flaherty.

"She had decided she would rather go out and do something about it," Judge Smith said.

4

WOMEN LAWYERS

In the fall of 1973 when Jenny Maiolo and Geraldine Ferraro were part-time lawyers and full-time house-wives, they met in Maiolo's law office to send out invitations for a bar association Christmas party. Both women had recently put in applications for jobs in the Queens County prosecutor's office, and while stuffing envelopes they talked about their upcoming careers. "Gerry then was exactly as you see her now—no different. Confident, sure that she could make things happen all the while convincing you that if you joined her you could too. She has that way of talking—'I've got to do it, we're gonna do it, come on, let's show 'em.' Well, Gerry was convinced that once we became assistant district attorneys a whole new world would be opening up for us. And just to make sure we would be ready, she insisted that the two of us go on a cottage cheese diet."

Maiolo, now a successful criminal defense lawyer in Queens, remembered, "Gerry certainly was right about our lives changing once we joined the D.A.'s office—even if I didn't stick with the cottage cheese and she did—but several months later she had another prediction, and this time I wasn't so ready to believe she would come through. It was nineteen seventy-four and here was Gerry telling me she was going to be the first woman President of the United States. President. A woman? From here—out of Queens? If it was anyone but Gerry I would have just laughed it off. But as I was walking out the door I remember thinking to myself, 'Is there any way she could actually do this?'"

Ferraro had been used to the odds being against her, and when nothing is possible, suddenly everything is. She went to law school at a time when little more than 2 percent of the nation's lawyers were women. On applying to Fordham Law School her friend, Father Lawrence McGinley, then president of Fordham, sternly warned, "I hope you're serious, Gerry. You know you're taking a man's place." Ferraro recalled, "Unfortunately, that was always the attitude. You had no business being there, so if you insisted on staying you had better be good." She was, and when Geraldine Ferraro presented her academic record to job interviewers, they told her it was gender not ability that was holding her back. A partner at one Wall Street firm admitted he had asked her down for an interview simply because he was interested in seeing how a woman would handle herself under tough questioning. At the respected Wall Street law firm of Dewey Ballantine, Ferraro managed to survive five successive interviews. "Then a senior partner sat me down and said, 'Miss Ferraro, you're terrific, but we're not hiring any women this year.'"

At a time when criminal law still was considered an all-male province—the United States Attorney for the Southern District of New York was refusing to accept women for his Criminal Division and only a handful of women lawyers were working in county prosecutors' offices—Geraldine Ferraro insisted on trying out for the office that carried the reputation of being the toughest and the best: "I received a job offer from the Office of the District Attorney of Manhattan and there too went through four interviews, culminating with one with the great man himself, Frank Hogan. I was called and offered a job. I advised the office that I could not start work until September, as I was getting married two days after taking the bar in July and would be going to Europe on my honeymoon. I received a phone call back several days later rescinding the job offer. A major concern was that training would take a certain period of time and being a woman, I would start to have babies and it would all be wasted."

Geraldine Ferraro took her bar examination in a segregated facility. It was not until the American Civil Liberties Union filed suit against the New York State Board of Law Examiners ten years later that women were permitted to sit in the same room as men for the two-day exam.

Ferraro passed the bar, but found, not unexpectedly, that the prospects for women attorneys in Queens were even worse than they were in other parts of New York. Fewer than a handful of women attorneys had ever been hired for the District Attorney's Office. No Queens woman had ever been appointed or elected to judicial office. A number of political clubs were segregated, with men's and women's groups meeting on separate nights. A prominent Queens law professor prided himself on separating his women students from the men, placing all the women in one class "so I can enjoy teaching the other one." Women lawyers were paid substantially less than their male counterparts, the excuse usually being "you're a married woman—you don't need the money" or in the case of single women, "let the guys buy you dinner." Women were absolutely prohibited from joining the eighty-four-year-old Queens County Bar Association, making Queens the very last county in New York State to bar the admission of female attorneys. For nearly thirty years, women lawyers in Queens operated their separate but not equal Queens County Women's Bar Association. They lobbied for passage of the Equal Rights Amendment and for funding for a separate Domestic Relations Court, operated the only civil legal aid program in the county out of a court basement on Union Hall Street, and offered mutual support for members who more often than not found male colleagues protective and patronizing. One member recalled, "At the time Gerry was admitted to the bar, you couldn't even say the men were hostile to us. Why should they have been? We weren't a threat to them, and they knew it. It was only when we started demanding our rights that we saw the attitudes change."

Spearheading the drive for equality that year was Marie Beary, now a New York State Assistant Attorney General. Insisting "they've kept us out long enough—why should we be second-class lawyers?" Beary filed a civil rights action against the all-male Queens County Bar Association. Beary's lawsuit caused a furor in the legal profession, and when she looked for support among longtime friends, it wasn't always there. "Every woman lawyer I knew agreed with my position, but there still were some who thought maybe it was best not to make waves. But I simply had to fight for what I believed in, and Geraldine Ferraro is someone who understands that." The Queens County Bar Association, as a result of the Beary action, amended its gender restrictive bylaws and began admitting women attorneys. Beary is convinced Ferraro will easily make the transition from Queens Boulevard to Pennsylvania Avenue. "When you're the type of person Geraldine Ferraro is, you don't let the improbability of a situation bother you. Queens is a marvelous training ground for national office. You have all the combinations needed—you live in a big city and yet this really is a small town. Women lawyers in Queens have always known that anything we want we have to fight for. We still don't have our share of judgeships and political appointments, and when Gerry headed our women's bar association, that was always her complaint. Sometimes I think it was easier for Gerry to get the nomination for Vice President of the United States than it would have been for Vice President of the Queens County Bar Association."

Constance "Bonnie" Mandina, a dean at the City University Law School in Queens, agrees. The first woman appointed to the Bar Association's influential judiciary committee, Mandina agreed to step up to the Association's Board of Managers on the condition that a woman take her place on the judicial selection panel. According to Mandina, the condition was agreed to but never met. "And we've yet to see a woman president or vice president of the association nearly twenty-five years after women were first admitted."

Bonnie Mandina is convinced that Queens women have a special sense of feminism that is more in line with the rest of America than it is with nearby Manhattan. "Women in Queens think and vote like other feminists, but their appearances and life-styles do not usually fit the feminist stereotype. Often they are professionals like Gerry who never forget that they are housewives and mothers too. This gives them a better understanding of the problems all women face." As Ferraro reminded a national convention of women judges in New York City two years ago, "Increasingly, the poor and powerless are women and children. If we as women don't look out for other women, who will? If we as women don't care what happens to women, it will not just be the waitress or the welfare mother who loses. It will be every one of us. Every one of us who thought when we made it, all women had it made. Or who thought, 'If I make it, it doesn't matter who else makes it.' It is too easy to divide the world into 'us' and 'them.' And it is far too easy for us— secure, successful, well-off—to become them. A simple thing—an illness, a divorce, widowhood, alcoholism, economic depression—could turn any of our hard-won gains into a struggle for mere existence. I didn't go to Washington to represent the women of

39

this nation. But if I won't, who will? I ran and was elected, not as a feminist but as a lawyer. And as a lawyer I can argue more effectively for equity and fairness for all people."

Ferraro's full-time legal career began in the Queens County District Attorney's Office where she quickly earned a reputation for being a tough and fair prosecutor. Annmarie Policriti, the current president of the Queens County Women's Bar Association, remembers Ferraro giving a particularly effective oral argument in an appellate court, then turning around and saying to Policriti, "Did I sound nervous?" "If she was nervous she never let it show. I thought the presentation was marvelous."

Policriti recalls that Ferraro had a special interest in encouraging the careers of young women lawyers and in seeing that women victims were treated with respect. "When Gerry and I worked together in the D.A.'s office, there weren't all the programs there are now for battered women. I'll never forget the time this pathetic woman came into the Special Victims Bureau on an assault and sexual abuse case. She had two little babies and was afraid to go home. We didn't have any idea where we could send her for shelter, and it looked like she would be wandering the streets unless someone took her in. It was one of the busiest days in the office, and here was Gerry, the Bureau Chief, inviting the woman to stay in her office while she did her work. What a scene. This distraught woman, two crying babies, Gerry handling her calls and in between helping to feed the babies. And she did get her a place to stay."

Policriti remembers it was Geraldine Ferraro who urged her to become active in the women's bar association. "Once women were admitted to the regular county bar, there wasn't as much support for the women's organization. It was becoming more of a social club than an activist group, and that was a shame since, as Gerry pointed out, women still weren't getting their fair share of judgeships or other appointments in the county. So Gerry brought me into the organization, and I was amazed to see how she turned it around. At one of the first functions I attended, the tables were only partly filled. But Gerry was single-minded about increasing the membership, and she drew in a lot of young women who were eager to work for the association. She set up a speakers program that made meetings more lively, and she pushed through support for the Equal Rights Amendment. There was no question that under her leadership advancing women to positions of power within the legal profession was a top priority. The young women she brought in stayed and brought in others. Our association is now thriving."

Even those who disagree with Geraldine Ferraro's views have good things to say about the woman herself. Bonnie Mandina recalls, "Gerry and I were leaving a political function and waiting for our coats in the cloakroom. I'm a strict environmentalist and Gerry always seemed to respect my views, but then I noticed she was being handed a fur coat. I decided not to say anything, but I was upset. Yet, how can you be angry at a woman who at that moment turns to you and says, "Bonnie, I swear every one of the minks that were used for this coat committed suicide."

Rosemary Gunning, who became an attorney in 1930 and was the first woman from Queens to be elected to the New York State Assembly, is a Republican-Conservative. While she is supporting President Reagan in the upcoming election, Gunning is enthusiastic about Ferraro as an individual and about the selection of a woman for Vice President. "At the time I was admitted to the bar, about the only office a woman could expect to run for and win in Queens County was dogcatcher. It wasn't just that you couldn't get into the bar association—when I went to court and again when I went to the legislature, it was automatically assumed you were a secretary." Gunning notes the vehemence with which many men are opposing Ferraro's selection and says she is amazed. "Why is it that when they question her qualifications it seems there is more to it than that, that what really is at issue is her being a woman?"

She admits she was approached by the Reagan campaign committee in New York seeking strategies for defeating Ferraro in the upcoming campaign. "I told them she's a sensible, agreeable person who will do her homework and can rise to any situation. We disagree on many issues, but I told them if they're smart they will treat her with politeness and respect. People resent it when a woman is treated unfairly. Besides, I have a feeling that if you attack Geraldine Ferraro, you can count on having quite a fight on your hands."

5

THE DECISION

Judge Frank Smith first met Geraldine Ferraro before he became a judge—while he was a city councilman. "I met her at a local [political] function. I was a former chairman of the New York State Young Democrats. I thought she should expand her activities beyond Queens. When she was in the D.A.'s office, we started going around to local and community groups out in Nassau and Suffolk. We went with a defense lawyer and would hold legal seminars. Then they'd talk about the importance of becoming a party member."

While Ferraro was working as a prosecutor, she also got back in touch with Mildred Snyder, a neighbor whom she had become friendly with during the fight to stop the Lefrak buildings. Ferraro wanted to join the thirty-first Assembly District Regular Democratic Club, and Mrs. Snyder was now head of it. "She did everything a new club member should do to pay her dues." Mrs. Snyder remembered. "She licked the envelopes, sent out flyers."

So Mildred Snyder and Frank Smith were two of the people Geraldine Ferraro asked to stop by her house on a Sunday evening in 1978.

"The question was whether Geraldine Ferraro should run for Congress," Judge Smith recalled. "Congressmen don't need to reside in the district they represent, so we were trying to figure out which seat she should go for—or if she should go at all." During the meeting, John Zaccaro sat quietly in a chair and said nothing. "Gerry wanted to see if she could get Millie's support," Judge Smith said. Once that was given, the remainder of the small group also gave their support. Toward the end of the meeting, John Zaccaro spoke up. "Okay," he said. "If she's going to run then she'll have all the money she needs. She won't take it from the organization."

As it turned out, James Delaney, a Democrat who had held the seat for sixteen terms except when he lost it once during the Eisenhower years, decided that he was going to retire after thirty-two years.

"She was prepared to go against Delaney," Nicholas Ferraro recalls. "Then, lo and behold, Delaney decides not to run. We like to think he was afraid of the name Ferraro. I guess he was just old."

Mrs. Ferraro thought her contribution to Democratic-club work warranted being considered seriously as a candidate. Mildred Snyder, who ended up being the only district leader to support Mrs. Ferraro, agreed.

The other Democratic leaders in the district refused to put her name in the primary. But despite her embarrassment, she decided to take them on.

"I drove her around in ninety-eight-degree weather," recalls Mildred Snyder. "Mostly, we got our signatures at Times Square Stores on Metropolitan Avenue (a local discount store). Ferraro hit that store and a Pathmark supermarket armed with her petitions and her husband. She begged people to sign her petitions, pleading, 'It doesn't mean you have to vote for me.'" She got over five thousand signatures on a nominating petition, many more than the one thousand five hundred necessary to get on the ballot.

Then Mrs. Ferraro did something unique in Queens politics. She campaigned full time. Until then, there had always been an understanding that one kept one's job and campaigned when one could—a little at night and on weekends. But she came out full force. And since she was severely understaffed, she formulated a very businesslike strategy.

"My husband figured out the top forty polling places in Queens because there were more than a hundred and we only had about eight people." Geraldine Ferraro went off to the most popular spots. "We had to think of a few gimmicks," said Mrs. Snyder. "So if she went to a Greek neighborhood, we sent her off with a young, handsome Greek. To an Italian neighborhood, we sent her with a handsome Italian." In addition, they always sent her off with Munchkin doughnuts from Dunkin' Donuts, and she handed them out as she introduced herself. "We've never eaten those doughnuts again," said Mrs. Snyder. "The car smelled of them forever, but many people remembered her as the woman with the doughnuts."

One of the people whom Geraldine Ferraro had turned to for advice when she decided to run was Mario Cuomo, then New York Secretary of State. "I had encouraged her to run, but I didn't know Manton was going to run for the seat," Governor Cuomo said. Thomas Manton was the Democratic party's official designee and one of two male opponents Mrs. Ferraro was up against. Cuomo supported Manton. "Tommy Manton had been with me in 'seventy-four," Cuomo said. In 1974 Cuomo had run unsuccessfully for Mayor of New York against Edward I. Koch. "I was pleased I was able to support somebody who had been with me when no one else was. She was very unhappy about it."

She also didn't forget it. When Cuomo ran for governor in 1982, Ferraro supported Koch. "She said she did that because I had not been with her previously. I wish she had just said that she preferred Koch. Most of my friends went with Koch. The irony is Tommy Manton, who I stood up for, went with Koch."

On the eve of the primary, Geraldine Ferraro received a telegram from the Federal Election Commission saying that if she did not pay back loans from her husband, she would be violating the election law. She ended up selling a building she owned in Manhattan to pay back her family.

In the Democratic primary, Mrs. Ferraro defeated

both Thomas Manton and John Deignan. She won the three-way primary with 53 percent of the vote.

On the night of her primary victory, she had her housekeeper, Ernestine, cook up a batch of fried chicken, and she headed over to the Democratic headquarters with a bottle of wine. By evening's end, the party regulars were behind her.

Mrs. Ferraro had used her maiden name professionally since shortly after her marriage. She has said on many occasions that she did so to honor her mother. To the New York City Board of Elections, however, she was Geraldine A. Zaccaro until the start of her first congressional campaign in 1978.

In October 1960, after she married John Zaccaro, she applied for admission to the bar as Geraldine Ferraro. She was admitted the next spring with a notation that she was also known as Geraldine Zaccaro. On voting records, she had used her married name as she did in other personal and family situations.

In the spring of 1980, she applied to the State Supreme Court in Queens to restore her maiden name, Geraldine A. Ferraro, on the registration rolls.

Mrs. Ferraro explained to the court that she had been "known in the legal community" as Geraldine Ferraro and wanted to amend the election records for "professional and business reasons."

"A few of us sat around a coffee table, and that's where we made the decision to go with Ferraro instead of Zaccaro," said Mildred Snyder.

The name Ferraro was certainly well-known in Queens. Nicholas Ferraro served as the Queens District

Attorney until the end of 1976 and before that was a State Senator representing part of the congressional district in which she was running. "I thought Ferraro was a better name; it flowed better. Ferraro had a better recognition than Zaccaro—that would be safe to assume," Carmine Parisi, the Ferraro campaign manager, said.

"People who don't understand it don't understand Queens," Mildred Snyder said.

Michael A. Nussbaum, a consultant to the Ferraro campaign, recalls: "She had always used Ferraro, so there was no reason to give that up."

"I never thought I was going to run for office," Geraldine Ferraro explained, but when she did, she decided that she simply preferred her maiden name.

6

THE TRIAL

When Gerry Ferraro took the assistant district attorney job, her life moved a couple of blocks away from the tranquility of Deepdene Road to Queens Boulevard, the wide, boring roadway that cuts between dreary apartment houses with Chinese restaurants and knish stores on the ground floors. On the east side of the boulevard there is the low red-brick Borough Hall, and next to it is the seven-story criminal court building. Behind it is the House of Detention for Men. The District Attorney's office is in the rear of the court building.

This was always a male world. The court building is the center of Queens politics. Queens never looked to Washington because in Washington the jobs were for engineers and energy experts, and required tests. In Queens, the county leader picked nominees for judges; the best prize was the plum one of judge's law secretary which he named directly. In the Queens way, both parties crossendorsed (meaning that both parties had to give their support to) a State Supreme Court judge. So when six or seven openings presented themselves, through retirements or deaths, the county leader had a field day. As the place is normally Democratic, that leader had the most judgeships to give. The Republican leader was given a couple in order to insure his crossendorsement of the Democrats. Upon being nominated by both parties, a candidate for judge had no true election to face. He had a fourteen-year term and a high salary. Plus, there were secretaries everywhere in his life, people picking up his check for him, and everyone calling him "Your Honor."

Queens County is divided into forty Democratic political clubhouses. Each has a male and a female co-leader. At meetings, the male leader votes and historically the female co-leader votes just as he does. In three places in the borough, the clubs are actually divided into male and female, just as the old parochial schools still have boys' and girls' entrances.

The club that concerns us is the Powhattan Democratic Club. Dennis Butler is the male leader, and Mary Anne Kelly is head of the co-club, the Pocahontas Club. This club meets in an old wooden building on Newtown Road in Astoria, and it was to this municipal cauldron that Gerry Ferraro went in 1974.

And it was in the Queens courthouse, in a criminal trial, that she got her hands on a career that was to become historic.

In order to really see what she accomplished as an assistant district attorney, one must go to Queens Boulevard eight years later when Ferraro is a legend, and her record is buried somewhere in the courthouse.

On the seventh floor of the criminal courts building, a clerk went to a computer and shook his head. "We got to do this the old-fashioned way," he said. "She was precomputer," explained Tom McCarthy, who works with the present District Attorney, John Santucci.

The clerk then announced that the files in question, the cases of Gerry Ferraro, were over in the old courthouse on Sutphin Boulevard in Jamaica. This courthouse, as opposed to the flat modern cipher on Queens Boulevard, has steps and columns and streets with trees, the way a courthouse should.

The county clerk, John Durante, a short, round man, was in his first-floor office. Once his daughter Joan was pushed into a judgeship by Nelson Rockefeller. Durante is a Republican. Now Durante was singing about Geraldine. The Italians' connection is deeper than political parties. He also presides over a system that once saw no women from Queens being forced on juries. "We sent them jury notices, but all a woman had to do was send it back with her name signed to it, and that meant that, as a woman, she didn't have to come. If a woman did want to be on a jury, she had to come here personally and sign up, and then the lawyers didn't want her because they said she was volunteering to send people to jail." It wasn't until 1975—1975!—that Queens was legally forced to make women necessities on juries.

One flight under Durante is a large file room filled with copying machines used by lawyers to copy tran-

51

scripts. A clerk behind a desk demanded our CA number. This is a criminal appeals case number. The number he was given, CA 223 of 1976, was the number of a case people have recently taken an interest in. It was a case involving arson that resulted in the injury of twenty-three New York City firemen. It was the case that made Gerry Ferraro in Queens.

The clerk, Matt Maniace, smiled. "Nobody became famous losing a case," he said.

It is also unique in American political history to have a national candidate with a trial record that can be looked up. As a rule, our Presidents and Vice Presidents don't learn about life in the criminal courts. On past tickets, only William Miller, vice-presidential candidate under Barry Goldwater, and Tom Eagleton, for a month the candidate under McGovern, had backgrounds in criminal court work. As both were men, nobody bothered to go into the files. As Ferraro is a woman, Maniace, the clerk, is busy pulling out files.

The case of the People of New York against Morris Feuerstein consists of four volumes of transcript. A defense lawyer now pored through the pages of transcript and picked out the salient parts of the case.

Here is what greeted a reader as she sat at a table in the basement of a court building in Queens and traced the rise of the first woman in American history to the nomination of Vice President.

PRELIMINARY CHARGE

(A jury was duly impaneled and sworn.)

THE COURT CLERK: This is indictment number 1752 of '76.

Let the record show that Morris Feuerstein is present with counsel, Melvin Lebetkin; Assistant District Attorney Geraldine Ferraro is present.

Jurors, as I call your name, please answer:
(*Whereupon, the roll of the jury was taken by the Court Clerk.*)

THE COURT CLERK: Twelve jurors and two alternates are present and seated in the jury box.

Madam District Attorney, you may open.

MISS FERRARO: Judge Browne, Mr. Lebetkin, Mrs. Laskey, ladies and gentlemen of the jury:

As you already know, I represent the People of the State of New York in this action against Morris Feuerstein. I must make an opening statement. I welcome the opportunity to do so, because I consider that probably one of the most logical requirements of all of trial practice. You see, the purpose of the opening statement is to tell you what this trial is going to be all about. It has been likened to the picture on top of a puzzle box that tells you what those pieces are going to end up looking like when you finish. It has also been likened to the index in front of a book that tells you what is inside. You pick your analogy. At least you have the idea of what an opening is.

The first thing I am going to do for you is to read to you from the indictment. The Judge has just done that, but I will do it again, and it reads:

"The Supreme Court, Criminal Term, Queens County; the People of the State of New York vs. Morris Feuerstein, the defendant.

"The Grand Jury of the County of Queens, by this indictment, accuse the defendant of the crime of arson in the third degree, committed as follows:

"The defendant, above-named, on or about May 28, 1976, in the County of Queens, State of New York, did intentionally damage a building by starting a fire."

The first thing I am going to tell you is what we are going to prove. The People will prove that on Friday night, May 28, 1976, Morris Feuerstein and his employee, Milton Kane, were working late at Jen West Bootery, a shoe store located at 37–07 82nd Street in Jackson Heights here in the County of Queens.

A few minutes before 9, Mr. Feuerstein told Mr. Kane to go, that his business was slow. And so, at five to 9, Milton Kane left the premises and left Mr. Feuerstein inside. A few minutes later, Mr. Feuerstein secured the premises and walked out of the store.

The People will prove that at approximately 9:08 he was still in the vicinity; that at approximately 9:10 the smell of smoke became obvious to passersby; that at 9:13, smoke was seen pouring out of the building; that at 9:24 the first alarm was in; and that by 9:48 the fire had raged with such rapidity that it had now reached a third alarm.

54

The evidence will prove beyond a reasonable doubt that the fire started in the bootery; that it was no accident; that it was incendiary in nature; and that the defendant, Morris Feuerstein, started that fire.

We will prove that only he had the access, only he had the means, and only he had the motive to destroy a heavily insured building.

When the trial is over, ladies and gentlemen, I will come back to you and I will review the testimony with you and you will see that I will have delivered every promise that I am making to you in this opening statement so when I do so, I will come back and ask you to convict the defendant, Morris Feuerstein, of the crime of arson in the third degree, as charged.

Thank you.

THE COURT: Counsel, you may open.

MR. LEBETKIN: Your Honor, Mrs. Laskey, Miss Ferraro, ladies and gentlemen of the jury:

Fortunately, a prosecutor in this country cannot get up and make a speech and convict anybody by her words—that is, without a trial. A prosecutor must present evidence; that is his or her obligation to you as a jury. And you have heard no evidence as yet.

In order to prove something, they must not only bring you witnesses, which I fully expect that they will bring you, but they must bring you witnesses who you believe, believe to be...

(During the trial, in her cross-examination of a defense witness, a retired fire marshal, Ferraro cracked the case by getting the fire marshal to admit, in the following sequence, that the fire had been incendiary.)

Q. Okay. Let's go to your testing of Afta. You heard Fire Marshal McCann testify that he could put a cigarette out in Afta; did you hear him testify to that?

A. Yes.

Q. Did you have the same reaction after your testing?

A. I didn't put a cigarette out in it.

Q. What did you do?

A. I put a lit match in it.

Q. You indicated also, I believe, on direct examination, that eventually you were able to get it to burn; is that correct?

A. With a piece of cotton, that's correct.

Q. And you indicated that it burned for a period of time, I believe; is that correct?

A. Yes—it was self-extinguishing—yes.

Q. You say it was self-extinguishing. What other combustible materials did you have around it when you tested that Afta to see if it could burn?

A. I did it outside. I wouldn't test anything at all inside. I had it in a metal plate, like similar to a pie plate.

Q. Yes?

A. And I put the Afta inside the plate, a small amount, covered the bottom—and that's the conditions.

Q. So then, actually, you're telling me that you had no combustible materials around, because a metal plate is not combustible, is it?

A. That's correct.

Q. If you had placed a lot of combustible material around that Afta—for instance, shoe boxes and tissue from shoe boxes—and had done the same experiment, what would have happened to that Afta and the shoe boxes that were around it?

A. It more likely would have lit.

Q. Would it or would it not have lit?

A. It would have ignited the surrounding—whatever combustibles were in the air.

Q. So then it is a material that can be used to ignite other combustible materials; is that correct?

A. Relating to starting a fire with this?

Q. That's right.

A. You possibly can start a fire.

Q. Yes or no?

A. (No response.)

Q. Can you start a fire?

MR. LEBETKIN: Objection.

A. Yes.

THE COURT: Overruled.

Q. Going to your investigation of the premises, what date did you say you were there?

A. August 26th.

Q. That's fully three months after the incident, isn't it?

A. Correct.

Q. Did you examine all of the stores involved—

MR. LEBETKIN: At this time, I have to interrupt and ask Your Honor to strike all this testimony, on the ground that, as you have said yesterday, there is no—

THE COURT: Just give the ground, counsellor.

MR. LEBETKIN:—you said there is no testimony about Afta used here, and you instructed then, and I'm asking that you do . . .

(In the following cross-examination, with Fire Marshal Lukowski, she was able to bring out that the fire burned down, rather than up as most blazes do, because the flammable liquid must have been present

and seeping through the floor, causing the fire to burn down.)

Q. Where on the rear of the store, on the part facing Horn & Hardart or the part facing Letwinger's?

A. Right, Horn & Hardart—

Q. And could you tell us—

A. Both areas, the whole rear of the basement.

Q. But you did look under the area?

A. Yes.

Q. And the adjacent wall connected with Horn & Hardart?

A. Yes.

Q. Could you find anything?

A. Yes. I found I was looking up at the holes, and there was—you could see through—not see all the way through, but you could see partially beams and whatnot. There was some evidence of fire there.

Q. That had come through?

A. Yes.

Q. Did the fire indicate that it burned from the top to bottom or from bottom to top?

A. From—may I look at these photographs?

Q. Absolutely.

A. (Referring.) The fire—it appears it came from the hole on the first-floor level.

Q. So it burned down; is that correct?

A. Yes.

Q. Now, tell me, Mr. Lukowski, how does fire usually burn?

A. Fire burns up.

Q. And what seeping through the floorboards could cause it to burn down?

A. Okay. Now—

Q. Just answer the question.

A. Under those circumstances, it would have to be some kind of flammable.

Q. You're talking about a liquid; is that correct?

A. If it seeps, yes.

MISS FERRARO: Could he take a look at People's Exhibit number 8, please?

THE COURT OFFICER: (Handing.)

THE WITNESS: (Referring.)

(Short pause.)

Q. Would you call that low burning, Mr. Lukowski?

A. Could you indicate the area that you're talking about?

Q. The area here and adjacent to the wall (indicating).

A. (Referring.) This area that's circled and over here (indicating)?

Q. That's right.

A. The corner, in other words?

Q. And the floor, yes; is that low burning?

A. (Referring.) It appears that some parts here are not burned; some parts of it would not indicate low burning.

Q. Do you see any low burning at all in that photograph?

A. In the entire photograph, yes, I see some low burning.

Q. Okay.

A. Right here on the edge of the shelves, on the other edge of the shelf, yes.

Q. Would you also say that the burns as reflected in that picture are even with the floor surface?

A. (Referring.) Yes, some charring or what appears to be darkening.

Q. Isn't it a fact—

A. I don't want to get—

Q. I'm sorry. I interrupted your answer.

A. That's all right.

Q. Isn't it a fact that it's highly probable that a liquid is used where you have burns of that sort, since other sources of intense local combustion, such as trash, would normally burn up?

A. That went over my head, the last part.

Q. Isn't it a fact that it is highly probable that a liquid is used when you have burning of that sort, since, if you have combustible materials, they would burn up, rather than burning along the surface of the floor?

A. Highly probable?

Q. Yes.

A. There's that possibility, yes.

Q. I think the word I used is "probability."

A. All right, probability. Perhaps there's a probability that that would be a case that you described.

Q. Before, when we were discussing percentages of damage, and you indicated that as far as the bootery was concerned it would not be great damage, if you took the whole store, not heavy damage—I think that was your testimony; is that correct?

A. That's right.

MISS FERRARO: Could you show him People's Exhibit number 2?

THE COURT OFFICE: (Handing.)

THE WITNESS: (Referring.)

(*Short pause.*)

Q. Have you ever seen that report before?

A. Yes; I saw that someplace.

Q. You have had an opportunity to peruse it, haven't you?

A. Pardon?

Q. You have had an opportunity to peruse it, haven't you?

A. Yes.

Q. That's a report of the structural fire; is that correct?

A. That's correct.

Q. And utilizing the code that Mr. Lebetkin referred to before, where he indicated the amount of damage in that code, could you tell us what number is reflected in that code?

A. Three.

Q. Which would indicate what type of damage?

A. Three, I believe, was 50 percent or heavier.

Q. Now, when that code number is reflected in the report...

A. I don't have the code sheet with me, it's not here.

Q. I'm sorry. You told us what the code was. When

it's reflected in that report, does it refer only to Jen West Bootery?

A. (Referring.) The bottom two lines do.

Q. No, that isn't my question. My question was: Is that a report just on Jen West Bootery or is it a report on an entire conflagration of nine stores on 37th Avenue—

A. Right, 82 through 82-10 37th Avenue and 37-01 through 37-09 82nd Street.

THE COURT: Just a moment now. Will have many more questions of this witness?

MISS FERRARO: Two more, and that's it.

THE COURT: All right.

Q. So that report, which reflects heavy damage, it is referring to all of the stores; is that correct?

A. Yes.

Q. And not just Jen West Bootery; is that correct?

A. Yes.

Q. In your opinion, having studied that report, would you call that heavy damage as well, all of those stores?

A. To all of these stores?

Q. That's right.

A. Yes.

MISS FERRARO: Just one other question.

Q. In all the fires that you have investigated and have called suspicious, have you ever called a fire incendiary without sending it out for chemical analysis?

A. Yes.

MISS FERRARO: No further questions.

THE COURT: Counsel, I presume that you will have some redirect?

MR. LEBETKIN: Yes.

THE COURT: Fine.

We'll take a short recess.

MR. LEBETKIN: I have an application.

(Gerry Ferraro's summation ran for many pages of transcript. But in reading it, one can hear this flat Queens voice; not the voice of the great star on the podium at San Francisco, but instead the person the Republicans must run against—a cold, demanding, tough Queens Boulevard Italian-Catholic conservative woman.)

(After recess.)

(Whereupon, the jury was returned to the courtroom by the uniformed Court Officer.)

THE COURT CLERK: Indictment number 1752 of 1976, case on trial continued.
All present.

THE COURT: You may sum up, Madam D.A.

MISS FERRARO: Judge Browne, Mr. Lebetkin, ladies and gentlemen of the jury:

On behalf of the People of the State of New York, I want to thank you for the time and attention that you have given to this trial during the past two and a half weeks.

You promised during the voir dire that you would give strict attention to the evidence as it is presented to you, and I think you delivered on your promise. For this, I thank you.

I feel obligated to mention our participation in this trial. I have always been in awe of his reputation as a defense attorney in this county, and I agree that that participation is well-founded. We are not in contest with each other, as he indicated; our styles are obviously different. We are just trying to do our job.

You are not to consider whether you think one is better or one worse; that's not an issue in this trial. All you are to consider is what comes from the witness chair and the exhibits during the course of this trial.

Now, you made me a promise at the beginning of the trial, and I made you a promise too. One of the promises was that I was going to come back to you and speak to you when the trial was all over and review the whole testimony with you. I am going to deliver on that promise now.

I promised that during the course of my reviewing

the testimony with you that I would prove to you four things. I didn't promise to prove motive, means, or opportunity, not at all. I promised to prove to you, number one, that there was a fire; number two, that it originated in a store owned by Morris Feuerstein and called Jen West Bootery; number three, that it was incendiary in nature; number four, that Morris Feuerstein started the fire.

If I failed to prove any one of those things beyond a reasonable doubt, you have an obligation to acquit this man.

I am going to go over the testimony with you, step by step, point by point, and see whether or not I have delivered on my promise to you. Okay?

The first thing I promised to prove to you is that that was a fire. Now, that is probably the most academic point that has come up during the course of this trial, because there is no denying that there was a fire, and there is no denying that there were nine stores involved. So my proof on that was really quite simple; you'll have to agree with that.

Let's get on to point number two: Did the fire originate in the store owned by Morris Feuerstein? In order to prove this...

It's very possible that that claim which Mr. Feuerstein put in the same night would have been honored immediately, and it's very possible that he'd have gone to California, having retired, having gotten rid of a business that was losing money and gotten rid of all of his debts and taken it easy; that's very possible.

Is he a victim, as he sits there? Sure. He's a victim of his own act, because now he's had to respond and it has cost him money.

Again, the other thing about him being out of work, that's not in evidence either. Remember, he did it, and he did it to himself.

I just have to comment for just one minute about the testimony of two witnesses—and I will try to be very brief. Those are Judy Feuerstein and Mrs. Feuerstein.

Mrs. Feuerstein testified—and she obviously was confused about time. Listen, it's her husband. Would I lie about my husband? Probably.

Judy Feuerstein got up, and she testified, and it was one lie after another. But she's his daughter. And if my father were alive, would I get up there and do the same thing? Probably.

But, ladies and gentlemen, let's go through her testimony. She lied when she said the phone call came through at 9:20 or 9:25. Could that possibly have happened, that someone would have called her up, an unknown name, and told her that the entire taxpayer was on fire when no alarm went in until 9:24 and 9:28? Check the reports, because I'm not sure of the time. Is that possible? No way.

Could she have seen her father coming from the driveway at that time, as she had claimed, and then, in the next breath, say, "Well, I was looking for my father?" You knew you had just seen him in the driveway.

As far as the inventory, she said she did all the bookkeeping. And yet, when reminded about the

68

accountant, she said, "Oh, yes, the other guy does do the books for us."

She described the smell of gas. The only person in the world that can smell gas. Not one of them smelled gas, not one of them.

She lied to you about the leaks in the roof. Maroney testified that the entire roof had been retarred in March. She lied about the inventory.

Now, you tell me, you tell me if any one of you could sit down and tell not only that there were forty-five hundred pairs of shoes, but the styles, the prices—now, ladies—and I address myself to the ladies, because this is a ladies' shoe store—you know how many different styles of shoes there are, and you know how the prices can vary. You tell me if she could have memorized that whole thing? Yet, with this phenomenal memory that she has, she can't remember her Grand Jury testimony.

Now, the purpose of the photographer to come up here was to show you what the girl testified to at the Grand Jury when she got up there and said that she didn't testify to that or didn't remember. This phenomenal memory that can take—I can't remember the number of pairs—four hundred pairs of shoes could not remember what she did last year as far as testifying.

Judy Feuerstein lied to you from the minute she walked up this aisle and went in there and raised her left hand. She lied to you all the way.

Did she accomplish something, despite her lies? They were obvious lies.

Did Mrs. Feuerstein accomplish something besides the confusion? Yes. What was hoped to be accomplished here? Don't let it happen. Do not sympathize. I beg you not to sympathize. You promised, when you took your oaths, that you would listen to the evidence as it came from that chair. That's all you are to consider.

If you find yourself in any way trying to sympathize because he has a wife, that he has daughters, then fight it by thinking about the guys who were injured, because they have wives and daughters too. Fight it by thinking about the people who have property and who had no insurance on their property. They have wives and daughters too. And fight it, ladies and gentlemen, also by thinking about that pizza guy who, but for the grace of God, would have been dead. He probably has a wife and daughter too.

So please, sympathy has no place in your deliberations, absolutely none. He gets no credit because he's white. He gets no credit because he's sixty-two. He gets no credit because he's got pressure problems. He has to answer for his act, just as any one of you would, just as any kid in the ghetto would; it's a criminal act.

If we have proven him guilty beyond a reasonable doubt, you cannot say, "I can't because of his age or because of his family." No, please, I beg you to remember your oaths as jurors.

I think that's about it; that's it. I've gone over the testimony with you, and I have pointed out what I believe was a point-by-point of whether or not I have proved this defendant guilty.

There is something else I said I would do, and that is that when I was finished with my summation I was going to come back to you and ask you to convict Morris Feuerstein of the crime of arson in the third degree, as charged. I now ask you ladies and gentlemen to do that.

Thank you.

The jury was out two days and came back with a conviction. Lawyer Lebetkin remembers looking at Ms. Ferraro as she packed her things and left the courtroom. He said to others that day, and they recall and he recalls saying it, that the word "future" crossed his mind.

Tom McCarthy, the communications director for the Queens District Attorney, went into his desk and came out with the handwritten notes that Gerry Ferraro made for the sentencing.

They read:

"as the court is aware, the defendant Morris Feuerstein was convicted arson after three week trial. Under ordinary circ, I do not make rec on sentencing because I feel this is the province of the court. But in this case I would like to be heard. The dfndnt is a 62 year old man who accrdng to papers submitted to court has high blood pressure and wife who reportedly had other medical probs. These facts, judge, tend to make MF a sympathetic figure—before the bar. But I feel that we cannot and must not lost perspecive because of them. (Facts) MF is much more dngrs crim than he appears. That MF commited an act in total disregard of life was evident by the fact that 23 firemen were

71

injured as a result of the fire he started. Thank God none was killed. That he committed an act in total disrgrd of prop is evidenced by fact that entire taxpayer of 9 stores was totally gutted putting owners out of businesses, some permanently. If one could find a shred of jutifctn for actions, this rec not be made. But age and high blood pressure just won't do. Insurance fires are destrying our city block by block. Soon borough by borough. This must be stopped. At this time the da recos that dfndnt MF be sntnced to incarceration for maximum period of time afforded by statute for his cnvtn of arson that is mimnium 5 and max 15."

Judge Kenneth Browne sentenced Feuerstein to three and a third to ten years. Ms. Ferraro handed the handwritten notes to Tom McCarthy after the sentencing in order to help him prepare the press release.

The next time Mel Lebetkin heard talk of the case, he was on Grand Avenue in Maspeth and a young man handed him a political flyer for Gerry Ferraro for Congress. The first item under her name said, "As a District Attorney, she convicted and put in jail the arsonist who injured 23 New York City fire fighters."

That day, Lebetkin remembered her in the case. He thought of Congress. For her? At the least, he decided.

7

THE FIRST CONGRESSIONAL CAMPAIGN

Running with the slogan "Finally, A Tough Democrat," Geraldine Ferraro opened an office on Queens Boulevard and began her campaign for the congressional seat in the Ninth District against former Republican New York Assemblyman Alfred DelliBovi.

She hired a staff at $1,500 a week and rented a storefront office for $1,250 a week. Three weeks of off-hour radio advertising cost $27,000 and a one-page advertisement in *The New York Times*, about $15,000. The final tab for her campaign was $252,000. Mrs. Ferraro had thought that only about $25,000 would come out of her own pocket, but that wasn't the way it worked. In the end she had to pay $170,000 by selling personal property and taking out two bank loans. Her husband and friends supplied the rest of the money.

To finance her campaign and resolve the complaint

by the Federal Election Commission that her husband had exceeded his contribution limit during the primary, Mrs. Ferraro took out loans and sold interests in a building and a mortgage to raise the $170,000. She reported total expenditures of $382,000, including $130,000 in loans and repayments. As of March 31, 1984, she was still owed more than $50,000 by her campaign committee. The Federal Election Commission said her 1978 campaign cost $514,000, but Mrs. Ferraro complained that the estimate was at least $130,000 too high.

Her campaign was a visible campaign, the likes of which Queens had not seen before. Andrew Stein and Robert Wagner, the sons of rich men, could battle it out for the Manhattan borough presidency with millions of dollars, but that wasn't the way things worked in Queens.

"I had never seen such a big campaign for a little, silly, Queens election. Her picture was in every one of those poster slots on the bus on almost every single one I rode," recalled Karen Berger, a Queens bus-riding lawyer.

To everyone, (with the possible exception of John Zaccaro), her first contest was the most fun. It was also the nastiest.

"It was so exciting," said Tim Flaherty, who worked with her on all her campaigns. "It was the toughest and the dirtiest. There were innuendos that she was a lesbian, having affairs, not a good mother, things being said about her kids being in private school." All in all, it sounded like a pretty standard Queens battle— good and personal. After all, in 1982 Queens was well-known for the handwritten posters "Vote for Cuomo, Not the Homo." And the innuendos being publicly spread about Ferraro were light compared to some of the things said over telephones about her.

Geraldine Ferraro tells the story of sitting in a town meeting where her opponent, Alfred DelliBovi, passed out a flier attacking her son John's enrollment at Choate, a prestigious prep school. "And my husband was sitting there with me," she once told an interviewer, "and I saw this little vein in his neck, never seen it before, going ba-boom, ba-boom, ba-boom, and said, 'I'm going to kill him. Let's get out of here.' And I said, 'If I walk out of here now, I'm finished. They'll say this namby-pamby girl can't take this guy. I'll handle it.'"

Timothy Flaherty remembers how she won the audience with her cool response to the attack on private schooling for her son as well as her two daughters. "I ask you parents here if you were fortunate enough to make good in this country, wouldn't you do the same? Don't you want better for your children?"

"Here's a classy lady and a bit of a creep," Flaherty said. She won them over. "It was a loud campaign, but we knew we were going to do it. I did more work for her than I ever did for myself."

"About once a week we had round-table discussion," said Mildred Snyder. "We sent out questionnaires to Glendale and other areas, asking what they thought were important campaign issues. That's how we came up with the idea for the zip code. We needed gimmicks. We needed to get her name known. The zip code thing worked beautifully."

Some of the residents of Ridgewood and Glendale shared a zip code with neighbors in Brooklyn, so their car, home, and life insurance was higher because they had a Brooklyn zip code. The residents in Queens had tried to get their zip code changed for years and years. Also, in Glendale and Ridgewood, the people are proud that they live in Queens.

"They had requested James Delaney (the Congressman who preceded Ferraro) to do that forever," said Mr. Flaherty. "It was the little nickel-and-dime stuff that over the course of the years added up. It meant a lot to them." And Ferraro knew it.

During the campaign, Ferraro went to the White House to see if the President could help her. She needed exposure. Carter sent his mother—Miss Lillian—off to Queens, and her visit generated the free publicity Ferraro needed. When Miss Lillian was asked what she knew about the candidate, she replied, "I don't know anything about her except that my Jimmy likes her." Geraldine Ferraro never forgot Carter's help. "I have a soft place in my heart for Jimmy Carter."

And in November 1978 Mrs. Ferraro went on to defeat Alfred A. DelliBovi, who ran on the Republican and Conservative lines, and has won handily ever since.

Her first committee assignments were less than exciting, but Mrs. Ferraro tried to make the most of her work for the House Post Office and Civil Service Committee. She immediately pursued a campaign promise, winning a seat on the Post Office Committee and successfully pressuring postal officials to grant a separate zip code to residents of Ridgewood and Glendale.

She was reelected in 1980 by defeating Vito P. Battista with 58 percent of the vote. He complained that she "was very clever" in appealing to special interests within the district, "talking about a post office in one area and in another she'd talk about abortion," but he could not recall any speech in which she had actually altered her positions.

Mrs. Ferraro won a third term in 1982 by polling 73 percent in a three-way race.

She ended her reelection race two years later with a $17,000 surplus. That year, she returned a $1,000 check from the Glendale Chamber of Commerce because it was from a corporate account.

By June 30, 1984, according to records filed with the Federal Election Commission, she had collected $167,000 toward a reelection race, the majority of it from political action committees.

Later in her first term, after being denied a seat on the tax-writing Ways and Means Committee but winding up on the Public Works panel, she also won a seat on the Budget Committee.

She pursued legislation of special interest to children, women, and senior citizens; was credited with getting federal funds for the city's Third Water Tunnel project and larger federal reimbursements to New York City for police protection of diplomats. She also echoed the special concerns of her highly ethnic district—from defending Soviet Jewish dissidents to denouncing Turkish policies, from opening a hot line in her district to provide updates on conditions in Poland to commemorating the contributions of German-Americans. In voting to condemn the Soviet attack on a Korean airliner last year, she paid special tribute to one of the victims—Dr. Michael Truppin, her family's physician for twenty-three years.

She concentrated on local problems that were important to her constituents—the noise from Kennedy and LaGuardia airports, the need for more customs inspectors, concerns about the trucking of radioactive materials through the city. In 1981 she publicly appealed to the city to repair a bump on the Queensborough Bridge and applauded its quick response a few weeks later.

"You had this instinct about her—that we created a superstar," recalls Michael A. Nussbaum, consultant to her 1978 campaign.

8

CONGRESS

"Even when she was doing Gristede's," Pat Durando remembered, the new Congresswoman was working while she stood over the meat counter and checked out the lamb chops. "She'd always throw a few questions at you."

"How's Denise and Diane?" Mrs. Ferraro asked.

"Okay, and how you doing with John the Terrible?" Mrs. Durando responded, inspecting some ground round.

"Good," Mrs. Ferraro answered. "Hey, Pat, what-tya think about this abortion thing?"

"I got news for you," Pat said, throwing the hamburger meat in her cart. "It's somebody's own decision. How's Donna?"

"Wonderful," Mrs. Ferraro said, and she pushed her cart down the aisle.

"She was always talking about the kids in between so you didn't even notice she was asking you questions. Anything she was working on, she asked."

During her first term, Geraldine Ferraro held a position on the Post Office and Civil Service Committee as well as the Public Works and Transportation Committee. Although she later concluded these committees would not get her far within the hierarchy of the House, she knew that in her first term she had to prove herself on the zip code issue so her neighbors would let her come back for a second term.

During her first term, Ferraro quickly proved that almost nothing gets in the way of work. Ronnie Eldridge, of the Port Authority of New York and New Jersey, once showed up for a meeting with Mrs. Ferraro with "two very serious men, very formal and macho." By coincidence, Mrs. Eldridge's daughter Emily was roommates with Donna Zaccaro at Brown University. Mr. Zaccaro had dropped Donna off at school and Mrs. Ferraro had not seen the dorm room.

Mrs. Eldridge and the men in tight neckties walked into Mrs. Ferraro's office and the men sat down, ready to discuss business. However, Mrs. Ferraro had one unfinished piece of business she wanted to attend to: "Excuse me, gentlemen. Mrs. Eldridge and I have something very important to discuss.

"So tell me," Mrs. Ferraro said. "What does the room look like?"

When Ferraro was first elected, her husband tried to commute to Washington. But he couldn't sleep in her little studio with its humming refrigeration, so he soon gave that up. She began to commute to Queens on Thursday nights when Congress was in session. On weekends the two were together, though Mrs. Ferraro's political life occupied most of their time.

Two years ago Mrs. Ferraro recalled how she described herself when she was first elected to Congress: "I described myself as a conservative, with a small c, Democrat. But as you look at my voting record, you'll find it just isn't so—and the reason it isn't is because no matter how concerned I am about spending, I have seen firsthand what poverty can do to people's lives and I just can't, in good conscience, not do something about it.

"I didn't go down to Washington to represent the women of this nation. I ran, and was elected, not as a feminist, but as a lawyer. I didn't go to Washington to speak for the poor of this nation. I am not a bleeding heart, a sob sister. My campaign slogan in 1978 was 'Finally, A Tough Democrat.' I represent a conservative, middle-class, hard-working constituency, and I went to Washington to represent them.

"Something has happened in the years since I went to Congress. I have come to recognize how People Like Us can become People Like Them, through no fault of our own, especially if we are women." And she came to the cause, she has said, only after realizing the economic hardships of single women supporting families. During her first campaign, she never mentioned the word feminist.

Her political evolution was reflected in how she was rated by special-interest groups.

Her ratings by the Americans for Democratic Action climbed from 74 percent in 1979 to 79 percent in 1983,

81

and by the AFL-CIO's Committee on Political Education from 89 percent to 100 percent. Her ratings by the Americans for Constitutional Action dipped from 12 percent in 1979 to 7 percent in 1983 and from the conservative Committee for the Survival of a Free Congress from 24 percent to 12 percent.

In Washington she created a record that opened doors for her to the highest councils of the Democratic Party. Still, despite her liberal voting record, the first Congresswoman from Queens and now the first woman vice-presidential candidate picked by a major party rarely forgets what she describes as the "very, very conservative voting patterns" of her district.

In June 1984 she voted against the controversial immigration reform bill that was approved by the House. She said she did so because the voters back home did not like the idea of giving amnesty to illegal aliens. She voted for the bill to create a federal holiday to commemorate the birth of the Rev. Dr. Martin Luther King, Jr., but she did not sponsor the bill, because her constituents, 84 percent of whom are white, took a dim view of the measure.

However, she is at odds with most of Glendale and Ridgewood when it comes to abortion, the one issue that has followed her from her first campaign through to the present.

In June 1979, six months after she was sworn in, she took the House floor and stated that:

"The intensity of the movement against my position on this issue is so great now, I hate to think what it will be like as the election approaches."

GERRY! *(UPI/Bettmann Archive)*

Gerry at age twelve with her brother Carl. *(UPI/Bettmann Archive)*

GERALDINE ANNE FERRARO, B.A.

English

Propensity for modern novelists . . . "Gerry" . . . a breeze of practicality freshening academic pursuits . . . sparkling green eyes visualize the world with interest . . . definite opinions . . . vivid short story writer, — Hemingway's no competition . . . P.S. 158 claims her as their "Miss Brooks" . . . knitting from argyles to afghans . . . delights in the unexpected.

Her senior year photo as it appeared in the 1956 yearbook of her alma mater Marymount Manhattan College. *(AP/Wide World)*

Geraldine Ferraro being admitted to the U.S. Supreme Court in 1978.
(From the author's collection)

Working on the Carter/Mondale campaign.
(Santi Visalli/© The Image Bank)

Congresswoman Ferraro on Capitol
Hill. *(Santi Visalli/© The Image Bank)*

With New York City Mayor Ed Koch. *(© P. F. Bentley/Photoreporters)*

With New York State Governor Mario Cuomo. *(AP/Wide World)*

At the Solidarity Sunday March for Soviet Jewry.
(© P. F. Bentley/Photoreporters)

The Congresswoman at work. *(© P. F. Bentley/Photoreporters)*

Geraldine Ferraro and family at their Queens, New York, home.
(Santi Visalli/© The Image Bank)

With son John, Jr. *(Santi Visalli/© The Image Bank)*

The happy family. *(© P. F. Bentley/Photoreporters)*

"Even while shopping, she'd always throw a few questions at you," noted a Queens neighbor. *(© P. F. Bentley/Photoreporters)*

The Congresswoman cooks.
(Santi Visalli/© The Image Bank)

Presidential hopeful Walter Mondale with running mate in Minnesota. (© *Tannenbaum/Sygma*)

Speaking to the National Organization of Women. (© *Randy Taylor/Sygma*)

With some of her strongest supporters. (© *Randy Taylor/Sygma*)

The vice-presidential candidate at a picnic in Minnesota.
(© Hemsey/Gamma-Liaison '84)

Strategy meeting with candidate Ferraro and aides. *(© J. L. Atlan/Sygma)*

It's official—Gerry is his choice. *(© Walker/Gamma-Liaison '84)*

The triumphant nominee at the Democratic National Convention.
(© 1984 Dennis Brack/Black Star)

Speaking at a fund-raiser for the Democratic National Committee.
(© P. F. Bentley/Photoreporters)

The candidate congratulated by her mother.
© *P. F. Bentley/Photoreporters)*

Gerry! A Woman Making History. (© *Tannenbaum/Sygma*)

She said her colleagues might be inclined for any of three reasons to eliminate federally funded abortions for the victims of rape and incest.

"The first is religious. But this country is based on a separation of church and state. As a Catholic, I accept the premise that a fertilized ovum is a baby. I have been blessed with the gift of faith, but others have not. I have no right to impose my beliefs on them. I firmly believe, given my current situation, that I could never have an abortion. I am not so sure, however, if I were the victim of rape and faced with a pregnancy question, whether or not I would be so self-righteous. I do know that if either of my daughters were raped I would give them the right to choose what they should do."

The second reason is financial, which she described as "absurd and specious," given the cost to society of an unwanted child.

"The final reason is political expediency. It is easy to placate a special-interest group which is flexing its political muscle. It is the easy vote, I repeat, but not the courageous one.

"I ask you to be personal about this vote, because no crime is as personal as rape. I ask you if your wife or sister or daughter were raped and became pregnant, would you not give her the right to make her own decision? Would you not want to help her straighten out her life and forget?

"When you vote on the Obey Amendment, I ask you to do so in terms of a statement to your wife, your daughter, or your sister, because your vote is more than an abstract religious or ethical statement. It is a statement to those you love, telling them how you would view them if they were to become victims of rape."

Years later, she told a Planned Parenthood meeting that she considered herself "more pro-family" than those legislators who oppose free choice on abortion. "I believe that such legislation represents the most blatant form of federal intrusion into our most private lives," she said.

Last January, at a hearing of the Abortion Rights Mobilization, she said, "Because of my religious convictions and my personal feelings as a mother, I see abortion as a terrible, unfortunate last resort. But I am not prepared to impose those beliefs on all the women of America, especially those too poor to make their own choice."

To those who ask how she can reconcile her religion with her stance on abortion, she says: "I'm a Catholic. I go to church and take my religion very seriously. I say if I became pregnant I wouldn't have an abortion. I'd be a crazy middle-aged lady, but I wouldn't. If I was raped, I don't know what I would do, and if my daughter was raped I don't know what she would do."

Her mother tried to persuade her to change her view. "My mother said, 'If you run for the Senate, you've got to change your position.' I said I don't believe in abortion but I can't impose my belief."

On the Budget Committee, of which she is one of three New Yorkers, Mrs. Ferraro has learned much about the economic status of women. She is a sponsor of the bipartisan ten-part Economic Equity Act and the author of two sections that deal with reforming private pensions for women that would allow a homemaker to deposit as much as her spouse in an individual retirement account.

On the House Public Works and Transportation Committee, she often finds herself pushing construction projects favored by New York City. Lately she has been battling with the panel's chairman, Representative James J. Howard of New Jersey, who has tried to force New York to stop polluting the Hudson River.

During Ferraro's extraordinary rise in the House, she ran for and won the job of Secretary of the Democratic Caucus. She also became a member of the Policy and Steering Committee. And in the fall of 1980, she called her friend Frank Smith and his wife and said, "You've got to come out to Fire Island. The President's calling me."

"So Agnes and I went out to Fire Island, and it was a beautiful day," Judge Smith recalled. And the call was held up. And everyone started grumbling. Judge Smith thought he could have stayed home in Queens and sat on a deck. Here he was, right on top of the beach, and he couldn't go to it because he had to wait for this phone call from President Carter.

Finally, the President called. And everyone stood around the phone, staring at it, while Mrs. Ferraro, who held the receiver up in the air so they could all hear, said, "Yes, sir, Mr. President," and she accepted the position as National Deputy Chairman of the Carter-Mondale reelection campaign.

And Frank Smith, who moments before was grumbling that he wanted to go to the beach, has never forgotten that he heard the voice of a president.

Ferraro also briefly chaired the Credentials Committee during the 1980 Democratic National Convention and was elected Secretary of the House Democratic Caucus that December. She was also one of three Congresspersons named to the Hunt Commission on delegate selection the following July before becoming chairman of the committee drafting the 1984 platform.

She aggressively zeroed in on the chairmanship of the platform committee. She wanted it badly. "If they're looking for a woman for the Platform Committee and they are, they've got to have someone who can handle it and who wants it. If they're looking for someone who can handle it well, they're looking for me." She got the post in January and handled it well.

Ferraro had "deliberately sat it out" when she heard that the party wanted someone uncommitted to a presidential candidate to head the Platform Committee. When she was first asked what position she would like, Ferraro said she wanted to chair the convention itself.

"I figured that if I was turned down for convention chair, I'd be in good position to get the platform, because I knew they'd be thinking, 'Well, Gerry didn't get her first choice,'" which is what happened. "Some might call it calculating," she said. "No, I didn't set out four years ago to get the platform chair. It just so happened it worked out that way. And damn it, you pay your dues for a leadership position. You do your work, you do it well, and you don't step on anybody else in the process of doing it."

Ferraro has a higher than average party loyalty score, voting with a majority of House Democrats 92 percent of the time in 1983. In 1978 she supported the party position 78 percent of the time.

Her influence in the House has been helped considerably by her friendship with Speaker Thomas P. O'Neill, Jr. "Tip is a person I confide in a lot," she said. "We have a personal relationship. The men in my district are just like him."

With the Speaker's help this year, she relinquished the less important Post Office Committee and won a seat on the Budget Committee. Until recently, she referred to O'Neill as "one of the two men in my life."

But she split for a time with the House Speaker last September when she opposed a resolution allowing Reagan to keep U.S. Marines in Lebanon until early 1985. Her own son, John, was nineteen at the time, and she'd been to Beirut and talked with the young Marines. "I'm a *mother* and I *saw* those kids over there," Ferraro said. "When we had the debate, Tip came up to me and said, 'Gerry, you're with me, aren't you?' And I said, 'No, Mr. Speaker.' And he said, 'Gerry, you're part of the House leadership.' And I said, 'Mr. Speaker, I just can't.'"

It was just the kind of vote her district would have gone for. Mention military in most of Queens, and the men run out in their uniforms, carting duffel bags, and the women cry and wave the American flag.

On another occasion Ferraro wanted to attach an amendment to pending transportation five-cent gas-tax bill and was getting nowhere. She then decided that under a procedural prerogative, she could kill the bill and with it would go a million-dollar project in O'Neill's district. She made O'Neill aware of the prerogative, and she got her amendment. And O'Neill liked her strategy. "I've been legislating that way for thirty years," he said. "You did a good job."

Legislatively, Mrs. Ferraro had concentrated most of her energies on economic issues, especially those that affect women. She is a force behind the Economic Equity Act, a bipartisan package designed to address the economic problems of homemakers and women who work outside the home. She has worked with the Congressional Caucus for Women's Issues to draft two of the twelve bills in the act.

This year Mrs. Ferraro voted for the leadership's budget package. But of the major alternatives available, she voted only for the Congressional Black Caucus's budget, which called for large real cuts in the level of military spending and large increases in domestic spending and taxes. On the House floor she said she did so because "it is the only budget that we will vote on in the budget process that makes a serious effort to ease the suffering that has been inflicted on the millions of poor Americans, especially women, children, and the elderly."

She has been open about her lack of experience in foreign policy. In 1982 she told an interviewer, "Give me weapons and I don't know one from the other. Give me law, women's issues, or the budget." However, she has opposed funding for the MX missile, B–1 bomber, Reagan's *Star Wars* concept of space-based defense, and the production of nerve gas. Very much in line with her Queens constituents, she has spoken out about the need for a strong defense and supported funding of the Trident nuclear submarine, Pershing II nuclear missile, and draft registration.

Last December she acknowledged that she was "still not happy" with her grasp of foreign affairs. She has paid her own way to visit the Middle East, Taiwan, and Japan. She also went on a congressional trip to Central America.

Judge Smith recalled the vacation he and his wife, Agnes, took with Mrs. Ferraro and her husband last year. "In Taipei she ran all over the place. She did more work there. She visited prisons. Checked garment factories."

In Hong Kong she didn't go in search of bargains. Instead, she spent a full day getting briefed about the ultimate reversion of Hong Kong to mainland China in 1997, months before its fate was headline news.

9

STIRRINGS OF PROTEST

> *"We hold these truths to be self-evident: that all men and women are created equal; that they are endowed by their Creator with certain unalienable rights; that among these are life, liberty, and the pursuit of happiness. . . ."*

Elizabeth Stanton proclaimed that manifesto on July 19, 1848—exactly one hundred and thirty-six years to the day before Geraldine Ferraro stood in front of cheering throngs in San Francisco to accept her party's nomination for Vice President. If a thread following the women's movement in America could be traced from Ferraro's magic moment back through the ERA fight, women's liberation, women flooding the work force in World War II, the suffragist crusade—most historians and feminists would say that it led back to here, to the Women's Rights Convention, which electrified the tiny, rural hamlet of Seneca Falls in 1848.

That July, a teacher named Lucretia Mott and her friend Elizabeth Cady Stanton, still smarting from the indignity of being refused seats at the 1840 World Anti-Slavery Convention in London because of their sex, called a gathering to address women's rights and voice their collective frustration. Speaking to a crowd that had been drawn together from fifty miles around on that pleasant summer morning, Stanton issued her own Declaration of Independence ("When, in the course of human events, it becomes necessary for one portion of the family of man to assume a position different from that they have hitherto occupied...") and attacked "the history of repeated injuries and usurpations on the part of man toward women, having in direct object of an absolute tyranny over her."

But the old order was starting to crumble. The tremendous expansion, industrial growth, and social upheaval of the United States before the Civil War were bringing women out of their cozy nests and into the world of men. Slavery was the hot issue of the day, and the abolition movement—which had radicalized Elizabeth Statnon—was giving thousands of women their first chance to organize, hold public meetings, and circulate petitions. In 1825 Scottish-born Fanny Wright, a freethinker and free-love advocate, became the first woman in America to publicly oppose slavery. She established a model commune for freed slaves in the wilderness settlement of Nashoba, Tennessee. In 1838, the National Female Anti-Slavery Society met in New York with eighty-one delegates from twelve states. To the abolitionist Theodore Weld, who had asked to chair the meeting, they sent the defiant message: "Tell Mr. Weld that when the women got together they found they had minds of their own, and could transact their own business without his directions."

Meanwhile, with the invention of the power loom and the spinning jenny, women had begun to enter the work force in droves (24 percent of all workers by 1850), most toiling in Dickensian sweatshops that, however horrible, gave them another arena for collective action. In 1845–46, Sarah Bagley organized the Lowell Massachusetts Female Labor Reform Association and led a strike to improve the lot of female factory workers; the effort was largely unsuccessful, but it set a pattern of labor activism for the future.

Among the urban middle class, the rise of Transcendentalism—with its emphasis on intellectual fulfillment—was stirring dormant hungers in housewives. "What women need is not as a woman to act or rule, but as a nature to grow, as an intellectual to discern, as a soul to live freely," wrote Margaret Fuller in *Woman in the Nineteenth Century*, *The Feminine Mystique* of its day. "If you ask me what offices women may fill, I reply—any. I do not care what case you put: let them be sea captains, if you will." Aspiring housewives could turn to role models such as muckraker Dorothea Dix, who in 1838 exposed the hellish conditions in prisons and mental wards and spurred national reforms or to Elizabeth Blackwell, the country's first female doctor, who set up a hospital for women on New York's Bleecker Street in the 1850s.

Still, in antebellum days, suffrage was still not a popular subject for discussion among women. The National Women's Rights Conventions, held annually from 1850 to 1860, concerned themselves instead with trying to reform laws governing property and the custody of children following divorce, and improving educational and work opportunities. But Lincoln's Emancipation Proclamation, the North's Civil War victory, and the Fourteenth Amendment, which extended to freed "male" slaves the right to vote, galvanized women's leaders like Stanton and Susan B. Anthony. In the 1870s their National Women's Suffrage Association, poorly funded at first and with a tiny membership, kicked off a fifty-year crusade of picketing and lobbying legislators to get women the right to vote. Suffragettes had to contend with a diehard opposition, typified by Senator Frelinghuysen of New Jersey: "It seems to me as if the God of our race has stamped upon the women of America a milder, gentler nature, which not only makes them shrink from, but disqualifies them from the turmoil and battle of public life," he quaintly declared. "Their mission is at home, to assuage the passions of men as they come in from the battle of life. . . . It will be a sorry day for this country when those vestal fires of love and piety are put out."

Along with the suffragettes, women's groups were springing up across America. In the cities, the YWCA and women's clubs initiated child-care and community health programs and tried to clean up filthy, overcrowded slums—transferring maternal instincts to the public sphere. The Women's Temperance Union, which started up in 1874, launched a polemical crusade to ban the bottle. In industry, rapidly expanding after the Civil War, Susan B. Anthony led the formation of protective associations of women factory workers in the 1860s and 1870s; the Knights of Labor began organizing both men and women on an equal basis in the 1880s. In the South, where Harriet Tubman's prewar Underground Railroad had become a legend, the KKK lynchings of blacks stirred up *Memphis Free Speech* editor Ida Wells and other black women in protest against white brutality and Jim Crow laws.

By 1913 the acceleration of the women's suffrage movement and the growth of the Progressive Party had resulted in women's enfranchisement in nine states in the middle and far West. Women's leaders such as Carrie Chapman Catt—Anthony's successor as head of NAWSA—and Alice Paul (who would later lead the fight to ratify the ERA) set their sights on a constitutional suffrage amendment. The seven-year fight was a bitter one.

Millions of women entered the work force during World War I, lending strength to their argument that they were competent enough to handle political responsibility. But at the same time, the prospect of a flood of new voters, many of them reform minded and apparently militant, solidified the opposition of the political machines, the railroad and oil company bosses, and the legislators in the Jim Crow South, all trying desperately to guard their status quo. But the tide was running against the conservatives. In 1918 President Wilson lent his support to the suffrage movement, and the same year the Nineteenth Amendment was approved by the House and Senate. On August 26, 1920, fifty-three years after the first state suffrage referendum was held in Kansas, and after two years of state-by-state struggle, the amendment was ratified. Twenty-six million American women could go to the polls for the first time.

The great struggle had been won. Equality at the ballot box was suddenly a fact of American life, and millions of American women were giddy with a new sense of social and political possibility. "Even the girls who knew that they were going to be married pretended to be considering important business positions," wrote Sinclair Lewis in the 1920 *Main Street*, capturing the can-do spirit of the time.

American politicians, frightened by the prospect of a tidal wave of reform-hungry voters, immediately began pushing through prowomen legislation to hold down the assault. Congress passed a $1.25 million health care bill benefiting women and children. Michigan and Montana instituted equal pay laws, and twenty states granted women the right to serve on juries. But by 1925 it became clear to politicos that women posed no threat to the power structure. They were certainly not voting as a bloc, many were not voting at all, and most followed their husbands' voting patterns. The momentum for reform sputtered to a halt.

By the time the twenties arrived, the status quo had changed little from the presuffrage era. The numbers of women workers had actually declined slightly from 1910 and most of those were blacks or poor immigrants mired in factory or domestic work. "The woman is nearly always the cheap and marginal worker," wrote labor expert Alice Rogers Hagan in the early twenties, "and she is expected by the public and employer to remain one." Domesticity was still touted as the key to happiness. In 1930 the Institute of Women's Professional Relations advised women college students to specialize in home economics and interior decorating to avoid competition with men. In government women were virtually invisible—and the exceptions tended to be politicians' wives or widows. Nellie Taylor Ross succeeded her late husband as Governor of Wyoming in 1924. The same year, Miriam (Ma) Ferguson campaigned for Governor of Texas after her husband was impeached for corruption, running with the slogan "Two Governors for the Price of One."

Women began to make important political strides during the New Deal era. FDR appointed the first woman to the cabinet (Labor Secretary Frances Perkins), the first female federal court of appeals judge, and the first female ambassador. First Lady Eleanor Roosevelt became an indefatigable activist for greater government participation by women (though she argued against the Equal Rights Amendment at the 1940 Democratic Convention). And Mary Dewson, of the Democrat's women's division, mobilized 60,000 female precinct workers to get out the women's vote. By 1940, however, twenty states still prohibited women from serving on juries, seven gave fathers superior child custody rights, sixteen denied women the right to make contracts, and eleven stipulated that wives could not hold their own earnings without their husband's consent.

Pearl Harbor was a watershed, bringing millions of women to work for the first time in a massive, wartime mobilization. In aircraft plants, the number of female workers soared from 4,000 to 310,000 between 1941 and 1943; thousands more enlisted in the uniformed Women's Air Corps. *Life* magazine featured a pigtailed pilot on its cover, and Rosie the Riveter became a national symbol. Reflecting the changing mood, a poll taken in 1943 showed that 60 percent of Americans now approved of married women pursuing careers, compared with the 80 percent who had opposed it five years earlier. "We are building up an entirely different social climate," proclaimed Jennie Matyas, a labor leader, in 1943. "What we didn't consider the nice thing to do after the last war will become the regular thing to do after this one."

But signs indicated that Maytas's forecast was greatly exaggerated: when the boys came home, they wanted their old jobs back—and the establishment was on their side. A southern Senator urged Congress to "force wives and mothers back into the kitchen" to insure jobs for the returning vets, and a movement had emerged against day-care programs, which had eased working women's burdens during the war. The *New York World Telegram* charged in 1947 that child care was a conspiracy of Communists who were operating out of "social work cells."

An article in *Life* magazine the same year called "The American Woman's Dilemma" captured the confusion and frustrations of middle-class, educated women in postwar America as they returned to the hermetically sealed life of the housewife after World

War II. For many, escaping from the home had given them an exhilarating sense of independence that now threatened to be dissipated as they bowed to age-old notions of "a woman's place." One-third of 1934 graduates of the best women's colleges confessed, fifteen years after graduation, to feelings of stagnation and frustration; 25 percent of women surveyed in a *Fortune* poll in 1946 said they would rather be men (3.3 percent of men said they would rather be women). "Choose any criteria you like," wrote Margaret Mead, "and the answer is the same: women—and men—are confused, uncertain, and discontented with the present definition of woman's place in America."

But as the exigencies of World War II had summoned women to the defense plants, the "baby boom" and the family exodus to the suburbs in the 1950s ordained a new, holy mission for them. The society that had canonized Rosie the Riveter, the girl with the acetylene torch, now sanctified the aproned, eternally patient housewives of *Leave It to Beaver* and *Father Knows Best*. Family and the home were back in vogue, and thousands of suburban mothers were engaging in an endless ritual of PTA meetings, school library work, and shuttling junior in the station wagon between his Cub Scout meetings and his trumpet lessons. "Modern man needs an old-fashioned woman around the house," declared author Sloan Wilson. *Newsweek* stressed the importance of the husband's job and urged women to be "model(s) of efficiency, patience and charm." And psychologists, advertisers, sociologists, and the media all praised the routine demands of suburban living as

98

providing the ultimate solution to postwar female malaise.

Still, all was not as placid as it seemed. In 1960 there were twice as many women working as in 1940—and the greatest growth in the labor force had been among well-educated wives from families with moderate incomes. In the South, the explosion of black protest, ignited by the Brown vs. Board of Education decision that outlawed "separate but equal" schools, was stirring up moral indignation among many oppressed groups and promising to blossom into an across-the-board movement for civil rights. And in 1962, a suburban mother and free-lance writer wrote a book that sent an electric shock through millions of housewives who had been lulled into a consumer-oriented complacency. Her name was Betty Friedan—and the book was called *The Feminine Mystique*.

10

LIBERATION

Betty Friedan, née Goldstein, arrived in New York City in 1944, two years after she graduated *summa cum laude* from Smith College in Northampton, Massachusetts. The daughter of a jewelry shop owner in Peoria, Illinois, she was a plain but vibrant young woman who had already been inculcated with the sense of difference and detachment that came from growing up smart, privileged, and Jewish in a midwestern town. "You're a little marginal," Friedan once recalled in her youth. "You're in, but you're not, and you grow up an observer—that silken curtain feeling."

At Smith College, a young Betty Goldstein found an exhilarating release from the rigid sexual roles that had marked her childhood. "It was a great, marvelous thing for me," she remembered. "At home I couldn't take six books from the library because my father didn't like to see me walking down Main Street with so many." Yet at the same time, she recognized in Smith a symbol of women's whole predicament in those years surrounding World War II: it was an ivy-covered haven for ambitious, white, upper middle-class women whose aspirations, kindled in an atmosphere of intellectual ferment, would be quickly snuffed out by the demands of wifedom and motherhood in America's suburban nests.

Betty Goldstein was not about to let herself be sucked into the homemaker's tranquil little world. After graduation, she headed off to the University of California at Berkeley, where for two years she pursued an advanced degree in psychology. But the pressures of the era were strong, and the next two decades saw Betty weighing values, searching for an emancipated mean between the rigorous social definitions of "a woman's place" and her own towering ambitions. She fell in love at Berkeley, gave up her fellowship, fell out of love, and came to New York with dreams of making it as a writer. She moved into a flat in the village with a group of other Smith and Vassar girls. In 1947 she married Carl Friedan, a director of small theater companies. By the 1950s, Betty Friedan was raising three small children in a "Charles Addams house" in suburban Rockland County, enjoying a kitchen filled with the latest appliances and a life that, superficially at least, resembled something out of *Father Knows Best*.

Still, there was that silken curtain—Friedan's sense of being both on the inside and the outside, regarding her own position and those of other 1950s American women with a sense of critical detachment. As a writer, she considered the boredom, the dashed expectations, the malaise of college-educated middle-class women like herself, and saw them being programmed by the mass media into a kind of dishpan drudgery focused on consumerism. Through some insidious process, this had become equated with fulfillment. In her ground-breaking 1963 book, *The Feminine Mystique*, she bitterly attacked the "sex directed" educators, advertisers, psychologists, and other shapers of American culture who professed the Freudian gospel that "anatomy is destiny." "The suburban housewife was the dream image of young American women and the envy, it was said, of women all over the world. She was freed by science and labor-saving appliances from the drudgery, the dangers of childbirth, and the illnesses of her grandmother. She was healthy, beautiful, educated, concerned only about her husband, her children, her home.

"In the fifteen years after World War II, this mystique of feminine fulfillment became the cherished and self-perpetuating core of contemporary American culture. . . . If a woman had a problem in the 1950s and 1960s, she knew that something must be wrong with her marriage, or with herself. . . . What kind of woman was she if she did not feel this mysterious fulfillment waxing the kitchen floor? . . .

"It is no longer possible to ignore that voice, to dismiss the desperation of so many American women. This is not what being a woman means, no matter what the experts say. For human suffering, there is a reason."

* * *

Strident, repetitious, yet undeniably accurate, *The Feminine Mystique* was an Emancipation Proclamation. It called upon women, urged them to cast off their dehumanizing shackles and take their place as equals with men:

"The suburban home is not a German concentration camp, nor are American housewives on their way to the gas chamber, but they are in a trap, and to escape they must . . . finally exercise their human freedom and recapture their sense of self. They must refuse to be nameless, depersonalized, manipulated, and live their own lives again."

The Feminine Mystique instantly became one of the most talked about books of the decade, selling seventy thousand in hardcover and one million paperback, and forcing millions of women to rethink their roles as complacent, subservient housewives—part workhorse, part china doll. Friedan had, as she put it, "broken through the mystique that says a woman's fulfillment is only in the sexual sense," and millions of women would no longer be the same.

That same year, another Smith College graduate, Gloria Steinem, was also casting a jaundiced eye upon the sexual map of 1960s suburban America. Steinem had grown up in the industrial slums of East Toledo, graduated from Smith a decade after Friedan, then spent two years in India.

In 1962 she published an article for *Esquire* called "The Moral Disarmament of Betty Coed" which examined the changing sexual mores of the college campus and presaged a turbulent future in which women would by no means accept motherhood as their ultimate destiny. "The real danger of the contraceptive revolution may be the acceleration of woman's role change without any corresponding change of man's attitude towards her role," she concluded. The next year, the slim, blond young woman donned an electric-blue Playboy bunny suit and infiltrated New York's Playboy Club, exposing the sleazy, carnal atmosphere in an article for the now-defunct *Show* magazine.

"I was pushed and tugged and zipped into my electric-blue costume by the wardrobe mistress," she wrote, "but this time she allowed me to stuff my own bosom and I was able to get away with only half a dry-cleaner's bag." The bunny piece created a sensation. Overnight it turned Steinem into an ogled-over New York celebrity ("the thinking man's Jean Shrimpton," raved *Time* in an article that doted on her lissome figure) and sent her from Manhattan penthouse to penthouse in a cocktail-party-filled writing career that temporarily distracted her from her true, and ultimately realized feminist calling.

While Steinem was bouncing back and forth in the 1960s between writing on tropical vacations and Cesar Chavez and the Poor People's March to the Mexican border, Betty Friedan was going well beyond her own revolutionary first step in defining female subjection and malaise. For millions of American women, she began to realize that attaining equality with men required far more than a ceremonial smashing of one's vacuum cleaner or dustmop.

"After I wrote that book," she recalled in a 1966 interview, "I got thousands of letters from women, *burdening* me with their discriminations. Do something, they said. They were frustrated. Washington treated Title Seven of the Civil Rights Act of 1964, banning discrimination among women, as a joke. . . . No women in top positions at the Equal Employment Opportunities Commission itself . . . outrageous. In 1965, after Johnson's inauguration, at a tea a young woman from Utah said, 'Why don't you form an NAACP for women?'"

The result was the National Organization for Women, which Friedan founded in November 1966. Short of funds, filled with clashing personalities, vibrantly alive, N.O.W. was determined, said Friedan during the week of its founding, "to break through the silken curtain of prejudice and discrimination against women, to hammer away at the seemingly immovable American psyche which stubbornly resisted the idea of women competing with men on their own terms." Its goals were revolutionary; not since the suffrage movement half a century earlier had a force of women appeared so dedicated to smashing the old social order. "In those days," claims Friedan, "it scared more women than it did men."

N.O.W. centered its fight almost immediately upon the passage of the Equal Rights Amendment, which had been languishing in Congress for decades until Alice Paul—eighty-two-year-old founder of the National Women's Party who had originally introduced the ERA to Congress in 1923—persuaded Friedan to carry the torch. It was a climactic decision: in the long, drawn-out struggle for ratification that followed, N.O.W. enlisted the support of dozens of other groups, from the AFL-CIO to the YWCA to the American

Jewish Committee, yet it never relinquished its position as a primary mover and shaker for ERA. N.O.W. continued to grow in exposure, and in numbers (from three hundred at its founding to 200,000 today) and power, and has remained at the forefront of the women's revolution that has changed forever the face of America's political, economic, and social landscape.

But in those heady years through the 1960s to the early 1970s, N.O.W. was by no means the only women's group to burst on the political scene. More and more women were rejecting the stay-at-home, hermetically-sealed life that most men still seemed to expect from their wives. Perhaps the most forceful of these groups was the Women's Strike for Peace, which began, rather implausibly, as a one-day "strike" by 50,000 women in sixty cities in protest against the Cold War. Like the Nuclear Freeze movement that has emerged during the Reagan administration, the Women's Strike for Peace had a deep concern that the icy standoff between the superpowers was an intolerable threat to life on this planet. It could almost be seen as the ultimate clash of the genders, in which the macho posturings of American and Soviet politicans and military officers—*male* politicians and military officers—were opposed by a passionate group of wives and mothers dedicated to life-affirming goals. Betty Friedan's *The Feminine Mystique* was still gestating; nobody had yet heard of the women's liberation movement. So the Women's Strike for Peace was a breakthrough event in which women began to assert themselves politically over matters of particular concern to them. "It was always a very subtle putdown, the attitude of men, that 'if women knew as much as we know ...,'" recalled Dagmar Wilson, a children's-book illustrator and the founder of the Strike, as she looked back ten years later. "We broke the terrible silence of women to say that we are here and we count too." Ann Swerdlow, the founder of the New York chapter of WSP, believed that Friedan's concept of "the feminine mystique" was in fact turned to the group's advantage. "We used the fact that we were housewives and mothers, women stepping out of our accepted spheres. We were doing a job of being good mothers by becoming involved in political action for the sake of our children's survival."

Although the Women's Strike for Peace was originally intended as a one-day event, it quickly escalated into a full-fledged movement that focused on three issues: the achievement of a nuclear test-ban treaty, the strengthening of the United Nations as a peace-keeping institution, and universal military disarmament. As the Vietnam War escalated throughout the 1960s and hundreds of thousands of young draftees were shipped off to distant jungles for a cause that more and more people viewed with skepticism and dismay, the Women's Strike for Peace grew. "When Vietnam came along, we certainly hadn't accomplished our original three goals," said Ethel Taylor, WSP activist, "but we knew we had to get involved." The Vietnam War pushed the group into a dramatic range of tactics. Groups of housewives suddenly became expert draft counselors and knowledgeable in the tactics of civil disobedience. They held sit-down strikes in Congress. They laid down in front of trains carrying napalm. They chained themselves to the White House. One leader, Mrs. Cora Weiss, in conjunction with other peace group delegates, travelled to Hanoi and successfully negotiated the release of nine United States prisoners of war. And more than fifty WSPers were imprisoned for their cause. "Women were willing to commit themselves to civil obedience in the hope that other women would identify with them," said one activist.

But throughout the 1960s WSP concentrated primarily on such attention-grabbing acts of protest, which many of its critics put down as naive, idealistic, and gratuitously condemnatory of government policy. Where, they asked, was the constructive side of the movement? Where were the alternatives? Gradually, the WSP leaders realized they had to go to Congress and work within the male-dominated, entrenched system. In 1970, when the Women's Strike for Peace's first national and political director, Bella Abzug, ran for the United States Congress, the movement for the first time officially endorsed a political candidate.

Bella Abzug didn't arrive on Capitol Hill in 1971 so much as she erupted. As meek and delicate as a New York City taxi driver, Abzug brazenly defied the Capitol Hill old-boy notions that lady Congresswomen—who numbered a mere 11 at the time—were meant to be seen and not heard. Yet if Abzug was stubborn, foul-mouthed, and opinionated—qualities never before manifested by women on the Hill—she was also deeply dedicated to the cause of the militant New Left. She boisterously led antiwar demonstrators on the steps of the U.S. Capitol and kept up relentless vocal assault on the war in the House chamber. Even her most intense detractors on the Hill changed their attitude toward her from utter contempt to grudging respect when in 1971 she unearthed an obscure, long-buried procedural tactic that compelled the Nixon White House to hand over to Congress the notorious "Pentagon Papers" which detailed America's buildup in the Vietnam War. "Even senior members have commented favorably on that piece of legislative skill," said one Abzug aide at the time. "And they don't like anything Abzug does."

Abzug was also the first woman to run for Congress on a women's rights platform, and through her six-year congressional career she never relented in her evangelizing for the movement. She spoke out strongly against nuclear testing on Alaska's Amchitka Island, and vocally supported better health programs and education and around-the-clock day-care centers. And she succeeded in getting a sex discrimination amendment added to the Public Works Acceleration Act although it was later vetoed by President Nixon. Gloria Steinem called her an "electrifying leader," and while her political career was apparently ended following a string of election losses—a senatorial primary in 1976, mayoral primary in 1977, and a bid for a House comeback in 1977—Abzug had plainly changed the face of American politics. No longer would women be instantly relegated to back-row obscurity for the duration of their congressional careers. She had proved that they could be as forceful, shrewd, and knowledgeable as their male colleagues.

* * *

The struggle to end America's long war in Vietnam galvanized millions of women across America. It gave them a cause to work passionately for, often putting them at odds with their husbands and propelling many of them to prominence as spokeswomen, activists, and political leaders. The late 1960s and early 1970s saw Jane Fonda—"Barbarella" herself—transformed from the raging sexpot of the Roger Vadim movie to a strident antiwar protester dubbed "Hanoi Hannah" by hawks. Her antiwar speeches on college campuses and radio broadcasts from North Vietnam enraged some state legislators enough that they tried to ban her movies. In December 1971, aroused by the volatile political climate, Gloria Steinem launched the first issue of *Ms*. magazine—a pioneering journal for the New Woman which abandoned the cosmetology tips and how-to-be-better-in-the-boudoir fare of *Cosmopolitan* and other women's magazines in favor of serious discussions of hot women's issues of the day: child care, balancing family and career, Vietnam, the Equal Rights Amendment, and the growing abortion debate. *Ms*. became a fabulous success and gave Steinem, editor-in-chief, a sense of fulfillment which had eluded her throughout the 1960s. "I was still divided up into pieces as a person," she recalled of that decade. "I was working on one thing and carried about another. Which I think is the way a lot of us live our lives. I'm lucky it came together."

The next year, 1972, Steinem joined forces with the two other prominent feminists of the day—Betty Friedan and Bella Abzug—and organized the National

110

Womens Political Caucus, a nationwide bipartisan effort to get women involved full time in politics. It rallied around the slogan "Women Make Policy, Not Coffee!" and encompassed a broad range of women, from Democrat Shirley Chisholm to Republican Lenore Romney, wife of George Romney, Secretary of Housing and Urban Development under Richard Nixon. The NWPC conducted regional workshops in political techniques, lobbied on Capitol Hill for a national program for day care and the Equal Rights Amendment, began throwing its weight behind various sympathetic candidates (it backed a Repubican businesswoman in the 1974 North Carolina Senate race, for instance, because Sam Ervin was a vehement opponent of the ERA, once telling a woman's group "God could not be everywhere, so he made mothers"). "For the first time since the women's suffrage movement," observed *Time* that year, "American male politicians are responding earnestly to women's demands: equal pay for equal work, simplified divorce and abortion, readily available day-care centers. By 1976, enough of a bloc may be formed to tip the balance in the presidential election."

At the same time, the growing force of the feminist movement in America was producing an inevitable clash of egos. In 1972 Betty Friedan and Gloria Steinem split bitterly over what Friedan saw as Steinem's championing of antimale "sexual politics." *The Feminine Mystique* author, who had the decade before argued so stridently for women to assert themselves as full human beings, now charged that feminism was in danger of turning into the female equivalent of mis-

111

ogyny and provoking a national backlash, thanks to "radical female chauvinist bores." She accused Steinem of "ripping off the movement for private profit" with her magazine. In 1973, hoping to quell a rising surge of man-hating in the movement, she said that "women are now strong enough to see men not a breadwinners, not as sex objects, not as enemies, but human beings and brothers." However, feminism's Jacobins, led by Steinem, were having their day in the sun, and Friedan's call for conservatism was shouted down. By the mid-1970s she found herself eclipsed by the more militant wing. "I was no match for Steinem," Friedan declared in *It Changed My Life*, her 1976 memoir. "I'm just an ugly little girl who can't deal with the realities of political power."

The nasty squabble between Friedan and Steinem merely served to distract attention momentarily from the two burning issues of the 1970s that did most to heighten women's sense of identity and turn them into a cohesive political force: the struggle for "freedom of reproduction" and abortion and the fight for the Equal Rights Amendment.

By 1968 abortion reform was at the top of virtually every feminist's list of priorities. By 1970, despite the vigorous opposition of the Catholic Church, reform laws had been passed in seventeen states, and over two hundred thousand women were receiving legal abortions each year, a 1,000 percent increase over two years earlier. The watershed came in 1973, when the Supreme Court, in a 7–2 decision, ruled in *Roe v. Wade* that women had a constitutional right to an abortion for at least the first six months of pregnancy. As

N.O.W., the Women's Political Caucus, the Planned Parenthood Federation of American, and other pro-choice groups acclaimed the Supreme Court decision as a triumphant advancement for women's rights, a broad spectrum of prolife groups began to attack it vehemently on moral grounds, claiming that abortion constitutes the murder of an unborn person.

The anti-abortion crusade was initially sponsored by the Roman Catholic Church. Its "Pastoral Plan for Pro-Life Activity," approved in 1975 by the National Conference of Catholic Bishops, initiated a drive to combat abortion through educational activities such as counseling women with problem pregnancies, and working on the political front "to ensure legal protection for the right to life." Other prolife groups sprang up outside the church, most significantly the National Right to Life Committee, whose ranks rapidly escalated into the multimillions and included Jews and Christians, liberals and conservatives. In Congress the anti-abortion drive was spearheaded by conservative Illinois Representative Henry Hyxe. Each year from 1976 onward, he successfully sponsored amendments to appropriations bills which succeeded in cutting off most federal funds for abortions.

Meanwhile, another battle was raging throughout the turbulent 1970s, one that would also carry over into the present. Persuaded by ERA founder, Alice Paul, in 1967 to push for passage of the Equal Rights Amendment, the National Organization for Women had mobilized its forces. In February 1970 twenty N.O.W. leaders disrupted hearings of the U.S. Senate

Subcommittee on Constitutional Hearings, demanding that the ERA be presented to the full Congress.

By 1972, thanks to Representative Martha Griffith's astute maneuvering, both the House of Representatives and the Senate had approved ERA by overwhelming votes, and the amendment was sent to the states for ratification by the necessary thirty-eight. Senators Sam Ervin and Representative Emanuel Celler set an arbitrary time of seven years for ratification; by the end of 1972, twenty-two state legislatures had ratified ERA.

It was an exhilarating—yet all too transient—moment after years of struggle. Not only had women finally achieved the constitutional right to an abortion, but the rampant discrimination that had kept them mired as second-class citizens—the inequities of pay, old-age and insurance benefits, access to training and advancement opportunities—seemed at last on the verge of being wiped out forever by an amendment that declared succinctly: "Equality of rights under the law shall not be denied or abridged by the United States or by any State on account of Sex." By 1975 passage of the Equal Rights Amendment had seemed all but certain: the AFL-CIO, America's most powerful labor organization, had endorsed the ERA, reversing an earlier stand. And twelve more state legislatures had ratified ERA, bringing the total to thirty-four of the thirty-eight needed. Polls consistently showed that its passage was favored by more than two-thirds of U.S. citizens. No longer would women be forced to protest inequality on a tedious case-by-case, state-by-state basis. For women across America, many of whom had felt themselves spiritually awakened by Betty Friedan's *The Feminine Mystique*, this was the constitutional sanctioning of their new sense of equality, their own Fourteenth Amendment to follow up Friedan's Emancipation Proclamation. But N.O.W. and other organizers had not counted on the strength and organization of an array of ERA opponents that included the fundamentalist Christian churches, the John Birch Society, the Mormon Church, the Moral Majority, the American Farm Bureau, Phyllis Schlafly's Eagle Forum and its spin-off, the League of Housewives. Gaining momentum as the decade progressed, the groups operated both within state legislatures and at the grassroots level to arouse people's suspicions about the ERA's implications. The fundamentalists may have started the drive's spread through their notorious "pink sheet," a one-page alarm printed on both sides of a pink piece of paper which appeared on the bulletin boards of churches. "Ladies, have you heard?" it began, showing an illustration of two women on the telephone. "Are you sure you want to be liberated? God gave you a beautiful and exalted place to fill. No women in history have ever enjoyed such privileges, luxuries and freedom as American women. Yet, a tiny minority of dissatisfied, highly vocal, militant women are determined to 'liberate' you—whether you want it or not. What is liberation? Ask women in Cuba. Castro 'liberated' Cuba! Remember?"

Distributed from 1974 onward by Women Who Want to Be Women—which later became Pro-Family Forum, headed by Lottie Beth Hobbs—the pink sheet recapped many of the anti-ERA themes: federal control over private lives and states rights, the death of the family, social decadence, socialist support, and the draft. Other groups quickly entered the fray. The Moral Majority claimed that N.O.W. stood for "nucleus of witches." Militant antifeminist Phyllis Schlafly was perhaps the most visible vocal force, linking the ERA misleadingly to abortion and conjuring up images of unisex toilet facilities, homosexual marriages, and women being drafted for combat duty—which charges N.O.W. itself abetted by suing to have women included in military registration. "People were literally led to believe their worst fears," said Oklahoma Senator Marvin York, a strong supporter of ERA. In addition to the conservatives' vocal attacks, there was a shameful lack of support for ERA from what N.O.W. leader Eleanor Smeal called "the invisible lobby of business" that profited from sexual discrimination. Neither the National Association of Manufacturers nor any other trade association, insurance group, businessman's alliance, or Chamber of Commerce made its voice heard in support of ERA.

Meanwhile, pro-ERA forces countered with a strong campaign that included highly visible demonstrations and educational literature aimed at allaying fears. In November 1977 more than 2,000 delegates, including Rosalynn Carter, Betty Ford, and Lady Bird Johnson, and 12,000 observers jammed into Houston Colliseum for a three-day National Women's Conference that established a detailed agenda for the coming decade. Five resolutions were dubbed controversial, high-priority "hot buttons," including ERA endorsement, a proposal for federally financed child care, a demand that government funds be made available for abortion, a legal end to discrimination based on "sexual and affectional preference" (namely, lesbianism), and the demand that President Carter establish a cabinet-level women's department responsible for guaranteeing equal rights. One year before, the deadline for ERA ratification, a N.O.W.-organized ERA extension march brought 100,000 supporters to Washington, the largest feminist march in history. Shortly afterward, the Congress agreed to extend the deadline by another three years, to June 30, 1982.

By 1979, however, the ERA was in desperate trouble. ERA opponents had successfully gotten five states—Kentucky, Idaho, Nebraska, Tennessee, and South Dakota—to overturn their ratification votes. And the more precarious ERA's position became, the more desperately inept its supporters seemed to become. In Illinois, according to *Time* magazine, a woman offered a state legislator a thousand-dollar bribe. In Georgia, another went one step farther, offering up her body in exchange for a vote. Florida legislators were roused from their beds at seven A.M. on a Sunday morning by strident ERA workers who banged on their doors to hand them leaflets. Zealous ERA supporters painted a state senator's driveway with ERA slogans and defaced the white dome of the state capitol with graffiti. Moreover, organizers of the ERA movement had made woefully few attempts to broaden their base among women beyond the white middle class, alienating nonworking women, minorities, "pink-collar" workers, and a growing number of upscale professionals in law, business, and medicine who had already achieved parity with male colleagues. In the end, ERA supporters'

117

moral fervor could not compensate for their political naiveté. "We all tried to tell them how the process worked and the importance of things like raising money," said Elaine Gordon of the Florida legislature, "but they didn't believe us. They thought that just being right would be enough."

By the year 1980, the position of women in politics and society had changed dramatically from the days before Betty Friedan, Vietnam, and the civil rights movement. Their numbers in the work force had doubled to over forty million a year in twenty-five years. Their proportion in the major professions had also risen. In 1970 only 4.7 percent of the nation's lawyers and judges were female; by 1980 that number had increased to roughly 10 percent. Women physicians rose from 8.9 percent to 12.8 percent in a decade, and women bank officials and financial managers climbed from 17.6 to 24.7 percent. Some 400 were sitting on corporate boards of director versus a mere 20 in 1972. And America's professional schools were turning out a steady pool of female talent in growing numbers. By 1980 one in five graduates of American business schools and one in four graduates of law and medical schools was female. Though still vastly underrepresented in politics, there were twice as many female state legislators as there were in 1971, and 90 women mayors of American cities that had populations of more than 10,000. Surveying the position of women from her lofty vantage point at the 1977 National Women's Conference, Betty Friedan declared: "Women have gained enormously over the last fifteen years. We have broken through the barriers, and it is more than just tokenism."

But the great strides told only half the story: the median salary for women by the late 1970s was still only 60 percent of that of American men, with a disproportionate amount of women still filling up pink-collar positions as teachers, clerical workers, and retail salesclerks. There were only seventeen women in Congress and no female Supreme Court Justices. Equal pay for equal work had not been achieved and the "hot buttons" of abortion and the Equal Rights Amendment, for which women had fought so hard for a decade, had fallen under a withering assault from the New Right. As American entered the 1980s, society found itself confronted with millions of independent women who had been politicized over the past two decades. Women had come out of their kitchens and from under the shadows of their husbands and formulated their own feminist agenda for the future, fully cognizant of their nascent political force. "It's the women who seem to be staking out the first set of positions," commented political pollster Patrick Caddell, "whether it's on quality of life or nuclear power, and the men who seem to be moving toward them. If that pattern holds up, it could be of enormous political significance. That changes the real dynamics of American politics."

At the same time, the tremendous growth of the women's movement had created a certain degree of self-doubt among many within the revolution itself, a feeling of uncertainty that promised to increase in the

1980s. The antiparent views of the radical feminist faction, who rejected the "tyrannical conventions" of the U.S. family in the early 1970s, had begun to seem a bit antiquated now. More and more women wanted children and found themselves torn between their maternal instincts and their career ambitions. Gone were the days of Ellen Peck's National Organization for Non-Parents, whose commitment to nonpropagation was succinctly expressed by the group's motto: "None Is Fun." Even Betty Rollin, who once wrote of motherhood: "A rude question is long overdue: who needs it?" had mellowed by 1979, when she said wistfully about her motherhood *manqué*: "I feel like I've missed something." Said New York feminist writer Ann Roiphe, author of *Up the Sandbox*: "We're seeing a whole rash of people having babies just in the nick of time. There's a difference between what one says at 20 and at 38. There's a swing back. All the excesses of the women's movement, including that one shouldn't look nice and so on are going to be sifted through."

One of the most prominent "sifters" was Betty Friedan. Repudiating her notion of motherhood and homemaking as "a comfortable concentration camp,' Friedan now affirmed the values of the family and called upon men and women to work together to balance careers and home lives. She bitterly accused radical feminists of alienating many women throughout the 1960s and '70s by exaggerating the man-hating, "sexual politics" side of women's liberation. "A lot was twisted and it began to be a repudiation of the family, throwing out the baby with the bathwater," she said in an interview. "They created the impression that the all-important thing was a career. They down-played the part of woman that is defined in terms of love and nurturing." Now, she said, women must move beyond the "first stage"—the attainment of a sense of identity and the downplaying of family concerns—and enter the "second stage": sharing family roles, developing flexible work hours, arranging maternal and paternal leave, and putting pressure on both the community and government level for expanded child-care services. Friedan's proposals, however, have been sharply criticized by many feminists, who suggest that many women still have not achieved the "first stage," and by such critics as the *Wall Street Journal*—which pointed out in a 1982 review that only 26 percent of all American homes contain two working parents.

Reaction of a different sort to the tumultuous change in women's roles was expressed in the best-selling 1981 book *The Cinderella Complex: Women's Hidden Fears of Independence*, by Claudette Dowling. Dowling's main thesis was that despite the militant asser-tions of identity by women in the 1970s—leaving one's husband, becoming self-supporting, living by oneself—women were still handicapped by their psy-chological dependence upon men. "Women are brought up to depend on a man and to feel naked and frightened without one," she wrote. "We have been taught to believe that as females we cannot stand alone, that we are too fragile, too delicate, too needful of protection. So that now, in these enlightened days, when so much has become possible, unresolved emotional issues hold us back." Dowling traced women's poor economic profile—two-thirds of women who work full time earn less than $10,000 a year, only 6.9 percent of all women are in managerial positions—not simply to male discrimination, but to most women's ingrained lack of self-confidence fostered in childhood and their craving for a dependent relationship.

This, then, was the state of American women as they entered the 1980s: they had made more strides politically, socially, and economically in the past two decades than in the whole prior history of the United States, yet they were still plagued by profound conflicts about the direction of their lives. Would the momentum built up during their crusades for equal rights be dissipated by the strength of the New Right, the comeback of the family, and by their own self-doubts? Or would they search for new, creative ways to balance motherhood and career while building their political base?

11

MOBILIZATION

In 1970 the Women's Strike for Peace had channeled its rage against the Vietnam War into a political force that sent Bella Abzug to the U.S. Congress. In 1982 women's mounting frustration with President Reagan was creating a mass mobilization across America. Tired of being outside the male-dominated government, they had begun to realize that the only way to achieve equality lay in sending their own representatives to the state legislatures and to Congress. "A flood of women candidates are coming out to run right now," said Louis Harris as he analyzed the effects of the gender gap in September 1982. "That 14 percent of women in state legislatures is going to change rapidly. There are going to be many more in all elective offices soon."

Betty Goetz Lall, a 1982 candidate for Congress from New York City's fifteenth District, typified the electrified mood of women voters. Four years earlier, when she entered the 1978 New York Democratic congressional primary, she had confronted a universal shrug of voter apathy. "An awful lot of people—men and women—brushed me off at subway stations," Lall recalled.

By 1982, however, times had changed. Lall won the Democratic nomination, boosted by a ground swell of enthusiastic female support. "I find that women are now very conscious of voting for women," Lall recalled that September. "That wasn't that much of a surprise to me on the part of younger women, but I talked to many older women too who said, 'The men have fouled up. We think women should have a chance.' Now, I find that when women focus on me at the subway or some other campaign stop and realize that I'm a woman running for office, they become interested. They ask me if I'm a feminist and when I say yes, they say, 'Okay, you've got my vote.' The women's movement has given a lot of women courage," she added. "A lot of people have been harboring thoughts they didn't articulate because they didn't think they were accepted thoughts. Now they are beginning to act on them. They saw the defeat of the ERA, and they don't want to accept that defeat. They also see the country's in a mess and needs new people. Look at the composition of Congress—it's 88 percent men."

Pollsters, activists, and politicians all agreed that the defeat of the Equal Rights Amendment in June 1982 had been a boon as well as a setback for women. "Before ERA," said Ruth White, Vice President at the polling firm of Yankelovich, Skelly, & White, "women didn't think of themselves as a power bloc. Women didn't necessarily vote for women candidates. But there's more feeling now that women candidates will be more sympathetic on certain issues. What's happened is that they've learned from the ERA failure that they have to have a power base. They've got to organize. They've got a long way to go, but they're gaining." The question now, said Denise Fuge, the President of New York City's N.O.W., had become: "Can you convert women who are in a movement for idealistic reasons—equal rights, abortions—to pragmatic politics? We'd never been able to do it. But when the ERA failed by such a narrow margin, women were furious. We know where the enemy is. They're in the legislatures. And we've got to change those faces."

In the weeks that followed the ERA defeat, the National Organization for Women, which had collected over $6 million for the ERA drive, moved quickly to channel women's frustration into results in the ballot box. "We're not going to be the cheerleaders on the sidelines anymore," proclaimed Eleanor Smeal at the news conference. She pointed out that in four key states that had failed to ratify the Equal Rights Amendment, 75 percent of the female legislators had backed ERA, versus 46 percent of the men. She called for women to kick off a political drive at the state and national levels, and urged the formation of "an independent third political force that will represent women's interests." Said G.O.P. feminist Kathy Wilson: "We can no longer be standing on the outside, wringing our hands over every roll-call vote. We have got to get women into office."

At N.O.W.'s national convention that year, feminist leaders pledged to intensify their campaign to outlaw sex discrimination in insurance, and to abolish the federal human-life amendment. They condemned "right-wing attacks on birth control, amniocentesis, and other reproductive rights." They promised to step up efforts to draw minority women into the organization and address the problems of family violence and disenfranchisement. And they vowed to defeat the Republicans in the polls in November. "The Republicans defeated ERA," declared Eleanor Smeal. "The vast majority of the opposition for reproductive rights comes from the G.O.P. side of the aisle." Showing a growing political sophistication, N.O.W. also endorsed Democrat Frank Lautenburg in the 1982 New Jersey Senate race, condemning Republican Millicent Fenwick—even though she had supported ERA—for her alliance with Reagan on budget cuts and military spending. "The Reagan economic program has done enormous damage to women," explained Smeal. "Money has become the excuse for slashing programs that comprise only a tiny portion of the federal expenditure. The administration, for example, doesn't believe in affirmative action, so it attacks it in failure to endorse regulations, in appointments and funding. They are trying to destroy it through the budget."

Armed with nearly 200,000 members, $1 million a month in contributions, 300 salaried workers, 6,700 full-time volunteers, and 750 phone banks, N.O.W. immediately set up a network of political action committees to aid federal, state, and local elections. Typical of the new local groups was "The Woman Power PAC" in New York, which endorsed and funded nine candidates for the city council and state legislature. A brigade of volunteers passed out buttons and T-shirts, manned telephones, did mass mailings, and raised over $20,000. In New York the Women's Political Caucus raised $5,000 for nine state legislative candidates, five of whom won their primary races. Noreen Connell, chairwoman of the Caucus, said PAC volunteers had been awakened and educated by the failed ERA drive. "A lot of our political activity was based on lobbying and pushing issues, and we learned a lot from that," she said. "But one thing we also learned was that you can lobby a Neanderthal for years and you're not going to raise his IQ. You've got to elect someone who's sensitive to the need for child care, domestic relations, and abortion rights. We discovered that a lot of state legislatures are really male locker rooms."

Political seminars for women were rising up across the country, offering public speaking workshops and campaign strategy sessions for novices and old pros alike. "Men normally come into the political area with a familiarity with public speaking from their business or professional lives," explained Mary Kay Long, executive director of the Connecticut Women's Caucus Research and Education Fund, a training and research group. "Women usually have not held the kind of jobs where the skills were needed. So they need extra training." Typical of the seminars was "The Effective Political Communicator," organized by the CWCREF, an intensive two-day course in August that brought together twenty Connecticut women who gave speeches, conducted mock press conferences, then watched themselves on videotape. Participants ranged in experience from a twenty-year-old Yale undergraduate to a fifty-six-year-old former Mayor of Hartford. All shared the perception that, as women candidates, they would be under special scrutiny to project an image of self-confidence. "To be taken seriously," said Sherry Deane, President of the Connecticut Caucus of Black Women for Political Action, "we have to be a little better than a man, because we still have to overcome certain preconceived images."

Meanwhile, the fears that women were better organized, better funded, and more inclined to vote Democratic than ever before had sparked change in the Republicans' strategy. As the 1982 congressional elections neared and polls showed that only 34 percent of women would vote for a congressional candidate who allied himself with Reagan, the G.O.P. began emphasizing "women's issues" and showing women in their televised advertisements. One of Illinois Governor James Thompson's ads opened up with an announcer proclaiming that Thompson was responsible for "the most extensive home nursing program in the nation." The camera showed an elderly mother and a daughter sitting together on the sofa. "My mother is eighty-five years old, and she is a diabetic, arthritic, and has a heart condition," the daughter said. "With Governor Thompson's program, she's able to stay in her own home and doesn't have to go to a convalescent home." In Michigan, Brooks Patterson, a district attorney seeking the Republican nomination for governor, was shown in a TV ad walking to a courthouse, accompanied by a female lawyer. The unspoken message, said ad maker Robert Goodman, was that "women are part of the action" in the Patterson administration. Senator John Danforth of Missouri, who had opposed extending the ERA-ratification deadline, now bestowed his blessings on another attempt to enact the amendment. And Republican Assemblyman Gill Gromley of New Jersey urged the State Civil Service Commission to reclassify jobs to achieve the feminist-supported goal of comparable worth. Far more common, however, were the indirect appeals such as the Thompson ad, reflecting the Republicans' belief that they were being hurt most by Reaganomics, arms buildups, and the threat of war, rather than the more narrow women's issues. One G.O.P. strategist warned his candidates: "Don't go on a rabbit hunt on ERA and abortions."

More women sought office in the 1982 elections than at any other time in American history. Fifty-six ran for the Senate and the House, 1,620 for the state legislatures. Women's groups had gained tremendously in power and prestige: in Colorado, office seekers who wanted the endorsement and support of the National Women's Political Caucus were compelled to answer twenty-four detailed essay questions that ranged in subject from rape to Social Security. "We used to have trouble getting people to fill them out," said Colorado NWPC Director Gerry Bean. "Now candidates are calling up and asking for questionnaires." PACs were burgeoning with donations from professional organizations of teachers, social workers, and nurses; the National Organization for Women had raked in a $3 million campaign treasure chest by election day.

In Michigan, where seventy-year-old Martha Griffiths campaigned for lieutenant governor, the one-time Democratic Congresswoman and passionate ERA activist was greeted with cheering crowds and standing ovations. Her presence on the statewide ticket helped pull her and Governor-to-be James Blanchard to a victory over the Republicans, convincing many that the time had come for a woman Vice President. Republican candidate Richard Headlee's sexist comments may also have contributed to his trouncing. Responding to changes in insensitivity to women, he pointed out that opponent Blanchard had only one child and remarked: "I have nine children. So who loves women more?" Jeered a local paper: "On that basis, women should prefer to vote for Peter Rabbit." In the Senate race in Missouri, Senator John Danforth, who was presumed to be unbeatable, was opposed and nearly unseated by State Senator Harriet Woods, a Democrat who is now running for lieutenant governor. Only tepid support for Woods by the Missouri Democratic organization, say some women experts, prevented her from winning. She had received virtually no campaign money until a poll taken two weeks before the election showed her gaining rapidly on Danforth. "The party decided it wasn't a winnable race," said N.O.W. President Judy Goldsmith. Still, all told, women gained one House seat and eighty-four in the state legislatures. And close races like Woods's, which Kathy

130

Wilson called "a moral victory," were an incentive to male-dominated party organizations to bring out their own checkbooks the next time around. As the presidential election loomed on the horizon, women felt confident that their days as political babes-in-the-woods were over. "Women once came into office to replace dead or indicted husbands, or because they were driven by a single issue," said Ruth Mandel, a professor at Rutgers University. "Now they look upon political careers as a real possibility. They are consciously, unashamedly in it for the long haul."

In 1984 the United States could boast 25 congresswomen, 86 women mayors in cities with populations over 30,000, and 992 female state legislators. If the figures were relatively small in terms of percentages, they still represented significant gains from a decade earlier when the numbers were 16, 12, and 425, respectively. More important, however, was the relatively sudden emergence of numerous female superstars on the political landscape—prompting both Democrats and Republicans to start talking seriously about a woman on the 1984 ticket. In San Francisco Dianne Feinstein had survived a traumatic recall vote led by a coalition of gun-loving "White Panthers" and homosexuals and won reelection in 1983 with a stunning 81.2 percent of the vote. Martha Layne Collins won a convincing 1983 victory in the gubernatorial race in Kentucky where four of the eight constitutional offices are now held by women. In the House, Democrat Patricia Schroeder and Republican Olympia Snowe, co-chairwomen of the Congressional Caucus for Women's Issues, took the lead in pressing for passage of

Economic Equity Act. Representatives Geraldine Ferraro, Lindy Boggs, and Barbara Kennerly wielded mounting influence on, respectively, the powerful Budget, Appropriations, and Ways and Means committees. Within the G.O.P., Kansas Senator Nancy Kassenbaum and Secretary of Transportation Elizabeth ("Liddy") Dole were constantly mentioned as Veep material.

Furthermore, it was gradually dawning on the American public that the qualities necessary for survival in the political jungle were not exclusively male. If a decade ago women politicans were stereotyped as Bellicose Bellas—loud, brassy, more suited to the Yankee Stadium bleachers than the House chamber—Geraldine Ferraro, Dianne Feinstein, and Nancy Kassenbaum were proving that femininity and strength could go together. Strict gender definitions had fallen by the wayside in the 1980s: macho had given way to "the new man" as sensitive Alan Alda succeeded Green Beret John Wayne as role model, and women could display ambition, power, and self-confidence without being viewed by men with instinctive hostility or suspicion. "Toughness," Dianne Feinstein pointed out, "doesn't have to come in a pinstripe suit."

In fact, female politicos were being regarded with equanimity in some of the unlikeliest places in America. Greg Dixon, spokesman of Indiana's Moral Majority, who once held that "God has made the woman, biologically and physiologically, keeper of the home," now asserted that he would encourage members of his organization to vote for a woman if she shared their spiritual values. "Our people would be more willing to vote for a woman who opposed abortion on demand rather than a man who supported abortion," he said. Phyllis Schlafly had no objections either. "I don't think the public cares," she shrugged. "They care more about policy." And in the bars of Chicago, oral historian Studs Terkel said that while locals may have ultimately turned on Mayor Jane Byrne, nobody was saying that it was the Mayor's "womanness" that had caused her troubles. "The issue is dead," said Terkel. "The guys in the bar are ready for a Gerry Ferraro, a Pat Schroeder, or a Barbara Mikulski." And a recent poll by Yankelovich, Skelly, and White discovered that though some sex stereotyping does exist among voters—the subjects saw men as good in a crisis and capable of handling rough decisions, while women were understanding, better organized, and good with details and new ideas—"substantial" numbers are ready to vote for a woman. The catch, however, says Florence Skelly, is that "if a woman's opponent has the same experience and the same stand, she's got a problem and is slightly disadvantaged."

Senator Nancy Kassenbaum (Republican of Kansas and the first female Senator who did not follow her husband into public office) typifies the progress that women politicians have made over the past two decades. Twenty years ago Kassenbaum, now fifty-one, was a mother and housewife preoccupied with raising her four children, who were born so close together that at one point all were under five years old. She served on the local school board, did some door-to-door campaigning for others in local races, and avidly read the newspapers, but "never, ever really thought of being an active candidate." After her children grew up and her marriage dissolved, however, Kassenbaum announced her candidacy for the U.S. Senate to succeed retiring James Pearson, whom she worked for for one year. "In a way," she says, "I'm sure I looked like Mary Poppins dropping out of the sky with her umbrella." Friends and political pros gave her little encouragement; her father, Alf Landon—the former Governor of Kansas and the 1936 Republican nominee for President against Franklin Delano Roosevelt—also advised her against it. "I think he worried about the publicity because my husband and I were separated, but he thought it would be very costly." Kassenbaum surprised everyone, however, and won the election—capitalizing on her name and the support of contacts at the University of Kansas.

Looking back on her first political campaign, Kassenbaum said that the key questions raised about her candidacy were, "Will she be tough?" "Will she be aggressive?" "I found that you don't have to be aggressive to be tough," she said. "It's knowing what you care about and your goals and your values that are important. If you have that, you indeed are tough."

She also faced initial skepticism in the Senate, where she found that sexism was deeply imbedded there. "It's the old-boy network," she told *The New York Times*. "It's difficult for a lot of men, just relating to a woman on foreign policy or the budget or some kind of political maneuvering. If you know what you're talking about, you gain credibility, but for women, you have to go the extra mile to prove your credibility." Kassenbaum, a moderate Republican, amply demonstrated that she *did* indeed know what she was talking about—and was not afraid to express views that sometimes put her at odds with the majority of her party. As a member of the Foreign Relations Committee, she worked out a compromise bill that reduced military aid to El Salvador. On the Budget Committee, she helped draft a plan that would increase taxes and cut back military spending, then joined eighteen Republicans in voting for the plan on the House floor over Reagan's objections. She gave her reluctant support to the MX missile, but urged the Reagan administration to work with the Soviets on arms control and has repeatedly warned fellow Republicans that the war and peace issue is widening the gender gap. "The sense in this administration is a heightened sense of militarism," Kassenbaum said. Her colleagues began to respect both her knowledgeability and her independence. "She came in here as Alf Landon's daughter," said one male Senator. "Now she's Senator Kassenbaum."

Across America the triumphs of women leaders over the Establishment and the old-boy political networks were pointing up the breakdown of the old social order. Secretary of Transportation Liddy Dole, whose parents once told her, "Well, it's your life," when she voiced her political ambitions, and whose Harvard Law School professor had declared one "Ladies' Day" a semester when he would call upon female students in class, now ran a 102,000-member Government Department and proclaimed that she was "on the cutting edge of a revolution." Pat Schroeder, another Harvard-educated lawyer, had received no support from the Colorado Women's Political Caucus in her winning 1974 campaign for Congress, because they felt it was "too soon" for her to run. By 1984 she had established herself as the most forceful spokeswoman on the Hill for women's rights. In Houston, feminist Kathy Whitmire, dismissed by her opponent as "that little lady," had surprised virtually all pundits in 1981 when she was elected Mayor in a city long known as a masculine bastion of beer-drinking good old boys, big-oil interests, and country-western music. "I think we've done much better in public life than anywhere else," said Whitmire, who has been nicknamed "Tootsie" for her uncanny resemblance to the Dustin Hoffman screen character. Clearly, the momentum was building toward the inevitable: a woman on the presidential ticket. But would it happen in 1984? With the Republicans firmly committed to the Reagan-Bush ticket, all eyes fell on Walter Mondale as the date of his San Francisco coronation approached.

12

THE GENDER GAP

The beginning of women's disenchantment with the Republican Party can probably be traced back to the 1980 Republican Convention in Detroit, when any hopes that the G.O.P. would endorse women's struggle for equality were soundly smashed. Encouraged by a 1980 poll, which revealed that a mere 43 percent of Republicans supported the Equal Rights Amendment (versus 54 percent of the general electorate), aides to nominee Ronald Reagan managed to push through, by a 90–9 vote, a platform plank that abandoned the party's traditional support of the amendment by declaring that the matter should be left up to the states. Next, North Carolina Senator Jesse Helms and his New Right battalions succeed in ramming through another bitterly contested plank that endorsed a constitutional ban on abortion. Many in the convention were appalled. "This will be very, very costly in political terms," predicted Michigan Governor William Milliken, a supporter of ERA. Former Republican National Committee chairman, Mary Crisp, who had just been ousted for her outspoken support of feminist concerns, accused the Republican Party of suffering from "an internal sickness." That November, in what many political pundits point to as the official emergence of the "gender gap," women showed, for the first time in history, a marked difference from men in their voting patterns. "Men voted for Reagan by a 56 to 36 margin while women voted for him by a 46 to 45 margin," pointed out Judith Neis in a *New York Times* piece. "Until 1980 there had never been more than six percentage points between men and women in a national election and that was only once—during the Eisenhower election."

By the early 1980s, Ronald Reagan's macho politics, his emphasis on heavy military spending at the expense of social programs, a deepening economic recession, and his hostility to ERA and abortion confronted a female electorate just waiting to be galvanized, and the results were explosive. Suddenly there was a whole range of women's issues which now seemed threatened by Reaganomics and his whole "less is better" governmental philosophy. "At the core of the Reagan program," explained sociologist Kurt Schlitchting, analyzing the gender gap, "is a call for the reduction of the role played by the Government in precisely those areas of traditional concern to women."

In a September 1982 survey, based on 4,058 interviews taken over a five-week period, Louis Harris predicted, with uncanny accuracy, the widening of the gender gap in the November elections. "The Reagan Administration is creating its own counterforce in American politics and women are right in the mainstream, right in the bull's eye," he said. "Women feel very keenly about the whole employment situation. Now, along with Blacks and Hispanics, they're in a last-hired first-fired situation. They feel they don't have equal opportunity for advancement nor comparable pay for the work they do. Women are worried about Reagan getting us into a war. Both men and women respond to jobs, ERA and the nuclear issue, but women are responding more." Harris concluded grimly: "Women are deserting the Republican Party in droves."

In a June 1982 column on the gender gap, Harris called the women factor in politics "one of the major developments of the 1980s. The undeniable fact is that women and men are voting differently and thinking differently on nearly all of the key issues that are likely to affect the power structure of this country." Gone forever were the halcyon days, the pollster said, when women clung meekly to their husband's shirttails. "In the 1950's and '60's and even '70's, it was a very common experience for women, a week before the election, to tell me: 'Well, I just can't say how I'm going to vote. My husband always sits down with me the day before and tells me who to vote for.'" Now, Harris asserted, as greater numbers of them enter the work force—from 26 to 53 percent in the last twenty-three years—women had become both far more independent and, to some degree, antagonistic to men. "Women feel that part of their problem is the way men

139

have treated them in a male-dominated society. They feel that foxes have been assigned to guard the chicken coop as far as women's rights and opportunities for women."

In 1982 Louis Harris conducted a nationwide survey that bared the deep ideological divisions between men and women and the growing disenchantment with Reagan's aggressive stance toward the Soviet Union. When the Harris survey asked people how concerned they were "that the world will be plunged into a nuclear war," men replied, by a 51 to 48 percent majority, that they were "not very concerned." Women, traditionally more antiwar and sensitive to human life (it was the Women's Strike for Peace in 1961, after all, that had taken an unpopular stand against arms buildups during the Cold War), said that they were "very concerned," by a 59 to 39 percent majority.

In economic matters too the gap was widening:

• By 60 to 37 percent, a majority of women were concerned that in the next year "more people will be going hungry in America," compared to a 52 to 45 percent majority of men.

• By 69 to 27 percent, a majority of women felt that "more factories will be shutting down" in the next twelve months, versus a 56 to 42 percent majority of men.

• By 73 to 23 percent, a majority of women were convinced that "more people will be losing houses and farms because they can't meet the mortgage payments." Men, by a 59 to 39 percent majority, expressed the same concern.

• Women, by a 63 to 23 percent majority, believed that over the next year "there will be even less new housing construction" in America. Men disagreed by a 52 to 46 percent majority.

• Women favored federal registration of all handguns by a 70 to 28 percent majority. Men favored registration by a 58 to 41 percent majority.

• Women favored affirmative-action employment programs for women and minorities by a majority of 72 to 20 percent. Men shared the same opinion by a 64 to 28 percent majority.

• By 87 to 10 percent, women favored the strict enforcement of air and water pollution controls, as required by the Clean Air and Clean Water Acts, compared to a 79 to 18 percent of men.

• By 50 to 38 percent, a plurality of women thought that women are discriminated against in the wages they are paid. Men disagreed by 49 to 42 percent.

• By 47 to 41 percent, women thought women are discriminated against in getting promoted to managerial jobs. Men disagreed by 47 to 43 percent.

Other pollsters questioned agreed with Harris that, in 1982 America, women were turning against the President. "It's been averaging about nine or ten points different between women and men," said Alec Gallup. "But ERA does not appear to have that much impact. The evidence shows it is not a terribly important issue with women. It is Reagan's image as pro-military that hurts him with women. They are concerned about issues like defense spending and nuclear war." Said Ruth Clark, a Senior Vice President at the polling firm of

Yankelovich, Skelly, and White: "Historically, women have been more attuned to the Democratic Party, more liberal, more concerned about the nuclear problem and the danger of nuclear war, more in favor of the rights of women to have abortions and obviously to gain equal rights. What's happening now is that women are suddenly aware of the fact that they have political power."

By the November 1982 elections, the policies of the Reagan administration and the defeat of the ERA had generated a new surge of power-brokering by women voters. The realization had dawned on them that they made up the majority of the electorate, that they could unite on a broad forum of issues that went beyond abortion and equal rights, and that the Republican Party was growing increasingly out of touch with women's needs and values. In 1983 that same realization was dawning on the White House as well. A story in the June 12 edition of *The New York Times* was headlined: "Vengeance Vote Worries White House," and contained an admission from White House political director Edward Rollins that women's perceptions of the G.O.P. as the "party of the men" could seriously damage Reagan's 1984 election chances. "It's a turning point in U.S. political history," Rollins acknowledged.

All the same, as the 1982 recession lifted and the American economy began moving again, Republicans were optimistic. Unemployment, inflation, and interest rates were dropping, easing the financial burdens of millions of Americans. President Reagan had begun to be viewed somewhat wryly in the press as "the

Teflon President." His policy in Lebanon, which resulted in the deaths of more than two hundred American Marines, his bellicose rhetoric toward the Soviets and the Latin American Marxists, the emergence of the "sleaze factor" in his political appointments, and his continued favoring of the rich at the expense of the poor all seemed to pale before his image of strength, self-assurance, and avuncularity. His popularity rating was soaring past 60 percent.

Women, however, remained largely unmoved. Looking beyond economic self-interest and unswayed by the big-stick heroics of the Grenada invasion, they continued to be angered by what they considered Reagan's antifamily, pronuclear stance. National security continued to be the single most divisive issue between men and women. According to Judith Neis, the gender gap had widened to a 20 percent on the subject as growing numbers of women felt compelled to find out all they could about Pershing missiles, SS-20s, SALT talks, nuclear fallout, "no first use" doctrines, and other forms of nuke-speak. "I think women feel that by not learning about nuclear weapons, we were like good Germans, enjoying an illusory safety through ignorance," one woman told Neis. Both the League of Women Voters and the American Association of University Women added nuclear weapons to their national agendas, and Dorothy Tidings, President of the League, spoke of the "amazing amount of interest in this issue" among her members. And the March 1983 issue of the *Radcliffe Quarterly* was entirely devoted to nuclear disarmament, featuring pieces by such distinguished Radcliffe alumni as historian Barbara

Tuchman (*The March of Folly*), Representative Barbara Kennelly, and Laura Nader, professor of anthropology. "I am increasingly hearing people say that Americans are being led down the path to a national Jonestown," said Nader.

Meanwhile, mounting attention was being paid to one of the most shameful consequences of Reaganomics: the "feminization of poverty" in America. Because women constitute the majority of recipients of public welfare, Social Security, and subsidized housing, it has been *women* who have suffered most by Reagan's devotion to the military budget at the expense of social programs. A recent report from the Children's Defense Fund reveals that since January 1981, more than 2.5 million women and 2.5 million children have fallen below the poverty line in America (now $12,000 for a family of four). Today, only 1 percent of women earn over $30,000 a year. The majority earn below $12,000 a year, and 85 percent of women over forty-five earn $10,000 a year or less. Women now constitute 61.5 percent of America's poor and 71.5 percent of America's elderly poor. And the vast majority have remained unaffected by the Reagan administration's economic recovery. As the Congressional Budget Office has pointed out, households with incomes above $80,000 have enjoyed benefit gains totaling $425 billion during the Reagan years, mainly in tax cuts. Households under $10,000—have suffered benefit losses of *$23* billion. Reagan cut $556 million from the Work Incentive Program, designed to help poor women move into the work force. He cut $2.9 billion from the social services block grant, cutting child-care services and forcing many working mothers to surrender their jobs and move onto the welfare rolls. He cut more than $3 billion from Medicaid—severely limiting the health-care services available to women and children—and cut away another $4.8 billion from the Aid to Families with Dependent Children, which provided support to female-headed households. "The people who've been hurt most are women and children," says Lynn Cutler, Vice Chairman of the Democratic National Committee, who has been raising her three children alone since her husband died. "Everywhere I go I see shattering scenes. By the year two thousand we will be nearly all the poor." Representative Barbara Mikulski of Illinois concurs with that grim forecast. Says she: "Reagan has done more to accelerate the feminization of poverty than any President in modern history."

In many other matters of concern to women, Reagan has shown indifference or, sometimes, antagonism. Just two days after his inauguration, Reagan met with representatives of the right-to-life movement in the Oval Office, a tacit endorsement of their goal to ban abortions. "It was a signal, because we were the first citizens' group in the White House," said Jack Wilke, the President of the National Right-to-Life Committee. "The one historic parallel is when the civil rights leaders were brought into the White House under Kennedy." Reagan's first Secretary of Health and Human Services, Richard Schweiker, was an ardent foe of abortion who proposed eliminating federal financing for the operation even in cases of rape or incest. He would allow funds only when the life of the mother was endangered. Reagan himself, while never openly calling for the passage of the Helms-Hyde Statute, hinted as much in press conferences. "I think what is necessary in this whole problem is determining when and what is a human being," he said. "Once you have determined that the Constitution already protects the right of human life. . . . Until we make to the best of our ability a determination of when life begins, we've been operating on the basis that, well, let's consider that not alive. I think that everything in our society calls for opting that they might be alive."

Reagan's critics also point to the President's unwillingness to tackle the issue of pay equity on a law-by-law basis. With American women now earning only sixty-two cents for every one dollar earned by American men, the past three years have seen a rash of lawsuits based on the newly established principle of "comparable worth"—that is, equal pay for dissimilar jobs of comparable value. The concept was upheld by the Supreme Court in 1981, when it ruled in favor of Oregon prison matrons who had been earning two hundred dollars less than deputy sheriffs guarding male prisoners.

Reagan has also held back his endorsement from the Economic Equity Act, a large package of bills designed to remedy inequities of pay and opportunity. The package, currently being debated by Congress, offers referral centers for families seeking day care, an end to insurance discrimination against women, and toughened procedures for collecting court-ordered child-support payments, nearly $4 billion of which went uncollected last year. The President is expected

146

to sign the child-support bill, which would take money out of the paychecks of negligent parents (90 percent of whom are men). But both Republican feminist Kathy Wilson and Democratic Congresswoman Barbara Mikulski charge that the signing is merely tokenism and that, in fact, the administration has done virtually nothing to advance most of the other legislation.

In nearly every department of government, feminists charge, the Reagan administration has pursued policies counter to women's interests. In 1983 Justice Department lawyers argued that the IRS could not deny tax-exempt status to a discriminatory private school, and proclaimed that abortion was a matter for elected officials to decide. The Justice Department was also the arena for one of Reagan's worst embarrassments: In August 1983 the Washington summer doldrums were suddenly lifted when Barbara Honegger, thirty-five, a Justice Department assistant, denounced as a "sham" Reagan's project to eliminate sex discrimination from federal laws and regulations. The next day, after resigning her $37,000 post, she lashed out at a variety of Reagan positions on women's issues, including his anti-abortion stance and the Equal Rights Amendment. The President "doesn't deserve loyalty," she concluded, "because he has betrayed us."

Honegger's startling *j'accuse* made her an instant heroine among feminists ("nothing less than Reagan's smoking gun on women's issues," said N.O.W. President Judy Goldsmith), and confounded administration officials already beset by worries over the election-threatening gender gap. The administration's counter-attack only exacerbated matters. Justice Department spokesman Tom DeCair dismissed Honegger as "a low-level Munchkin" and White House Press Secretary Larry Speakes smirked that "the last time I saw Honegger she was the Easter Bunny at the White House Egg Roll." Scorned Munchkin Honegger held a press conference ("Do you think they'd try to do this to a man?" she asked) and displayed a chummy photo of herself with Reagan ("This is the Munchkin with the Wizard of Oz"). Suddenly, Honegger was a media sensation with a crowded schedule of TV and newspaper interviews.*

Honegger's erratic performance in the limelight may have hurt her credibility (she announced plans to lead a demonstration in front of the White House which never materialized, rambled on about parapsychology to a *People* reporter, and arrived nervous, confused, and barefoot on Ted Koppel's "Nightline"), but the damage to Reagan's already tarnished image had been done. Shortly afterward, he agreed to support changes in 112 federal laws that discriminated against women; but even the Justice Department called the proposed changes—such as extending dining room privileges to the widows of the National Oceanic and Atmospheric Administration Uniformed Services Officers—"inconsequential." Nor were feminists impressed by the gesture. "Most of the changes he has agreed to are

*Joshua Hammer, as reported by Susan Deutsch, "Dream Banks, OZ and EST: The Strange Case of Reagan Rebel Barbara Honegger," *People* magazine, September 12, 1983.

meaningless exercises like changing the word 'widow' to 'spouse' in laws," said Pat Reuss, Legislative Director of the Women's Equity Action League. "The man is playing tuba on the sundeck while the *Titanic* is sinking. He doesn't understand the problem he has with women or else he thinks he can fool someone with his performance."

The same year, the Reagan administration was also wracked by scandal in the Environmental Protection Agency. A congressional investigation uncovered evidence of "coziness" of the EPA with industry, political cronyism, and lax enforcement of toxic-waste laws. One staffer had worked simultaneously for the EPA and private clients regulated by it, evading conflict of interest by not serving sixty straight days with the agency.

In December 1983 Rita Lavelle, the agency's Assistant Administrator in charge of waste programs, was found guilty by a federal jury of lying under oath to a congressional committee to hide her conflict of interest with the Aerojet-General Corporation, her former employer. And a witness quoted in the congressional report asserted that Reagan-appointed EPA director Ann Burford, had held up a $6.1 million grant to clean up the Stringfellow Acid Pits, a toxic waste dump in California, to hurt Governor Edmund G. Brown, Jr., in his campaign for the Senate. Mrs. Burford denied the charges—as did her former chief of staff, John Daniel—and no "smoking gun" was discovered, but Burford resigned in disgrace after months of intensifying pressure. "Criminal activity such as political manipulation and favoritism, while obviously bad, was far from being the most serious problems the Environmental Protection Agency presented to the American public," said one representative, a member of the congressional committee investigating the agency. "Far more serious was the degradation of environmental protection."

If Ann Burford was the Tweedledum of the Reagan administration's environmental team, James Watt was the Tweedledee. Owlish in appearance, self-righteous in demeanor, the Secretary of the Interior carried out his self-appointed crusade to exploit natural resources as if it were a holy *jihad*: he offered up record tonnages of coal in leasing public lands (the program was estimated to have cost the government more than $100 million), he announced a program to lease nearly all of America's continental shelf—nearly one billion acres—in 40-million-acre lots for oil excavation over five years. Outraged conservationists warned that chronic oil pollution from the drilling could devastate rich fishing grounds, and that oil rigs off Alaska could be wrecked by errant ice floes, spreading crude oil all over the fragile Arctic terrain.

But Watt remained blissfully unconcerned. He compared the conservation groups to Nazis who "want to control social behavior and conduct," and was as certain of his own righteousness as he was of his enemies' moral turpitude. "I want to change America," he declared, sounding like a Bible Belt evangelist. "I believe we are battling for the form of government under which we and future generations will live."

Of course, the Reagan administration's record on

women's issues is not entirely black. Feminists and Democrats—in fact, virtually everyone but the New Right—cheered his historic 1981 appointment of Arizona Federal Court Judge Sandra Day O'Connor to become the first woman justice on the Supreme Court, just two years after the Broadway play *The First Monday in October,* had toyed with the idea. Eleanor Smeal, President of the National Organization for Women, termed the choice "a major victory for women's rights." Miami Attorney Patricia Ireland, a regional N.O.W. director, pronounced herself "thrilled and excited," adding that "nine older men do not have the same perspective on issues like sex discrimination, reproductive rights or the issues that affect women's rights directly." Former Texas Congresswoman Barbara Jordan also congratulated Reagan. "The Supreme Court was the last bastion of the male: a stale dark room that needed to be cracked open," she said. "I don't know the lady, but if she's a good lawyer and believes in the Constitution, she'll be all right."

O'Connor's record, as it turns out, has justified neither the apocalyptic fears of the New Right nor the breathless optimism of the liberals. In most cases, she has allied herself with the conservative wing of the Court—led by William Rhenquist—but if not exactly establishing herself as a candidate for the presidency of N.O.W., she has remained a defender of women's rights. In the 1982 session, for example, she voted with the staunch majority in a decision barring employment discrimination in schools that received federal funds. Later, she ruled that a Mississippi state nursing school could not refuse to admit *male* students.

Her argument in that case was that not only were the male students being discriminated against, but that women nursing students were being stereotyped by the school's admissions policy. O'Connor has kept a low profile on the "hot button," abortion, although in a forty-five-minute meeting with Reagan prior to her 1981 appointment, she told him she found abortion "personally repugnant" and considered it "an appropriate subject for state regulation."

In a 1984 news conference addressing the gender gap, Reagan could also point to other achievements during his four years in office. He had appointed 1,400 women to positions in government—most prominently Secretary of Transportation, Elizabeth Dole, Secretary of Health and Human Services Margaret Heckler, and Deputy Attorney General Carol E. Dinkins, who now holds the highest position ever attained by a woman in the Justice Department. His administration has filed seven enforcement suits under the 1978 Pregnancy Discrimination Act, and has supported rounding up delinquent child-support payments. He has reduced taxes paid by married couples, changed the estate tax so that survivors (often wives) are not stripped of all their possessions, and has made it possible for married homemakers to open up IRAs in their own name.

However, women remain singularly unconvinced. In a December 1983 *New York Times* poll, only 38 percent of women surveyed believed that Ronald Reagan deserved reelection compared with 53 percent of men. Only 43 percent of women approved of his handling of foreign policy, and only 42 percent approved of his handling of the economy versus 57 and 56 percent of men. Most significantly, only 24 percent of women believed that the Republican Party is most concerned with fairness. Bella Abzug termed the President's attempts to "bridge the gender gap...cosmetic, callous and unconvincing." "The tax initiatives that Reagan had taken credit for," said Kathy Wilson, "are simply Congressional efforts that Reagan supported only after it became clear their passage was inevitable." In a profile in *The Washington Post*, Betty Friedan accused the President of "declaring war on women" and predicted that en masse, they would turn the tide against him in the 1984 election. "For the first time in American history," she said, "women have and will probably use their vast political power. Six million more votes were cast by women in the '82 elections than by men. Those extra votes are enough to elect a President and women are going to make the difference next time."

EPILOGUE

In Queens the phone call is already more famous than the one Alexander Graham Bell made to Watson. Walter Mondale called Gerry Zaccaro of Deepdene Road and asked her to be his running mate for the vice-presidency of the United States. And Queens acted in characteristic fashion: what's in it for me?

On Austin Street in Forest Hills, a few blocks from Geraldine Ferraro's residence, a hosiery store had a 20 percent discount on panty hose. Anywhere else that might be a good deal, but on Austin Street they jack up prices so much the buyer is still being robbed.

Over on Metropolitan Avenue the manager of Key Food swore to the national press and to every television station in the country that Mrs. Ferraro, the name most of the nation knows her by, has shopped in his store for twenty-four years. Some question whether the store has been there that long.

Over on Queens Boulevard Nick Jutis, the owner of a restaurant, has a sign in his window which reads: "In 1964, Nick Jutis, a waiter in Luigi's, bought this restaurant." Nick, who wishes he still was a waiter, said that there were many reporters around because in the main restaurant room, a dark place decorated in Queens Greek, was where Gerry Ferraro used to eat lunch. Doris from the OTB next door complained, "Well. They ain't writing me up." Nick said he thought that all the reporters should stay and write more about Gerry Ferraro.

And while Representative Geraldine Ferraro (Democrat of the Ninth District) may have eaten lunch at Nick's over on Woodhaven Boulevard, Joe Abbracciamento was fighting with the owner of the Spartan Restaurant on Grand Avenue in Maspeth about where Gerry was a regular. Mrs. Ferraro had to tell the press she wasn't a regular at any one particular restaurant. That's perfect. They'll plaster her picture in the window of every restaurant in the borough and they'll tell anyone who'll listen about her favorite dish.

On Deepdene Road, Gerry's home turf, Danielle Stockman hid from the five hundredth reporter to ask her what she thought about her now-famous neighbor.

"Please, no more questions," she said.

"What, is there bad blood between you?" the reporter asked. So for the five hundredth time, she told how much she liked Gerry Ferraro, which she really does. Some people who had had fights with her because she spoke her mind were announcing to the

155

world that Gerry Ferraro was a savior. People who hadn't spoken a word to her in years.

Mrs. Stockman had to beg her daughter Lisa not to be interviewed in her bikini. But it worked out okay because Lisa said there wasn't even one cute Secret Serviceman. Mr. Kramer was upset because people were parking in front of his home, unheard of on this little street. Everyone laughed at the reporter who asked if Mrs. Ferraro had been of particular assistance during the days when Son of Sam stalked the streets.

"Yes, she walked around with an Uzi," a neighbor said.

"Really!" he cried incredulously.

But Mrs. Ferraro moved on. As she always had done. She's already conquered Myrtle Avenue in Glendale and Ditmars Boulevard in Astoria. The rest is easy.

And, behind her each time, she leaves a door swinging while we race behind her, trying to squeeze through as many as possible. Each one she barrels through we catch just before it closes. Each time she makes it just a little bit easier. She's grabbed a little of the future and kept some of it for herself. Let's see what we can do with all that she's handed to us.

Appendix:

HIGHLIGHTS OF CONGRESSWOMAN FERRARO'S VOTING RECORD

ENERGY

For:

1979: An amendment to the Nuclear Regulatory Commission authorization bill to impose a six-month moratorium on construction of new nuclear power plants after the accident at the Three-Mile Island plant.

1980: Spending half of the revenues from the "windfall profits" tax on energy programs.

Against:

1979: An amendment to end "windfall profits" tax on newly discovered and hard to get oil in 1990 and to lower the tax rate on other types of oil to 60 percent.

THE ENVIRONMENT

For:
1979: Environmentalist-favored legislation to establish millions of acres of new national parks, wildlife refuges, and forests in Alaska.
1980: A proposal to give states the right to veto nuclear garbage-dump sites within their borders, unless vetoed by both houses of Congress.
1981: Halting funding for the Clinch River (Tenn.) breeder reactor.

Against:
1983: A proposal that would bar the EPA from imposing penalties on communities that missed a December 31, 1982, deadline for meeting clean air standards.

FOREIGN

For:
1981: A foreign aid appropriations bill.
1981: Blocking the Reagan administration's sale to Saudi Arabia of five sophisticated airborne warning and control system (AWACS) radar planes and other military equipment.

Against:
1979: Restoring formal relations with Taiwan.

1983: Increasing U.S. contribution to the International Monetary Fund to provide aid to developing countries already in debt.
1984: An amendment to authorize military, economic, and development aid for Central American nations in fiscal 1984–85.

THE MILITARY/DEFENSE

For:

1980: Aid for Nicaragua.
1980: Blocking the shipment of nuclear fuel to India because India would not agree to international safeguards on its nuclear power plants.
1980: Draft registration for nineteen- and twenty-year-old males, financed by transferring $13.3 million for an Air Force account to the Selective Service System.
1981: Deleting $1.8 billion in B-1 procurement funds. Deleting MX missile funding from the fiscal 1982 defense appropriations bill.
1982: Deleting $988 million for procurement of the first five production versions of the MX missile.
1983: Nuclear freeze on testing, production, and development of U.S. and Soviet nuclear arms.
1983: Ending covert U.S. aid to guerrillas fighting to overthrow the Nicaraguan government and substituting instead a program to openly help Central American countries to combat cross-border arms shipments.

1983: Deleting $2.1 billion to begin production of twenty-one MX missiles.
1984: An amendment barring testing of the antisatellite missile (ASAT) unless the Soviet Union tests its own ASAT after the bill is enacted.
1984: Deleting $21 million provided by the Senate for covert aid to Nicaraguan rebels.
1984: Barring money to build MX missiles unless Congress passes a joint resolution by April 1, 1985.

Against:
1979: A proposal requiring mandatory draft registration for eighteen-year-old males in the event of an international emergency.
1980: An amendment to delete $500 million from the Carter administration's $1.6 billion request for the MX missile to develop a deployment system to conceal the missile.
1982: Production of a new lethal chemical weapon.
1982: A proposal watering down a Nuclear Freeze resolution.
1983: Resuming production of lethal chemical weapons.
1983: Keeping U.S. Marines in Lebanon until early 1985.

SOCIAL ISSUES

For:
1979: A proposed constitutional amendment to ban busing to desegregate schools.

1979: A bill that included provisions to establish a national minimum benefit for welfare recipients and to allow unemployed two-parent families in all states to receive benefits.

1980: A spending plan that would add $1.1 billion to the first budget resolution for such programs as aid to cities, child health care, and mass transit.

1980: Key enforcement provisions in a bill to strengthen federal fair housing laws.

1981: Authorization of the legal service corporation, an organization that funds civil legal services for the poor.

1982: Overriding President Reagan's veto of a $14.2 billion fiscal 1982 appropriations bill that cut his request for defense spending and added social spending he did not request.

1982: An amendment to increase Medicare outlays by $4.83 billion while cutting defense spending by the same amount.

1983: An antirecession aid package to help unemployed homeowners meet mortgage payments and provide emergency shelter for the homeless.

1983: Adding domestic program funds to budget resolution for 1984 and reducing President Reagan's defense request.

1983: The Equal Rights Amendment to the Constitution.

1984: Removing certain wording from a child protection bill that would cut off federal funds to states that failed to report on alleged medical neglect of handicapped infants.

1984: Eliminating a ban on use of federal employee health benefits for abortion unless the mother's health is in danger.

Against:
1980: An amendment requiring better off recipients of food stamps to repay the government for the value of their stamps.
1981: Reducing individual income taxes and business investment taxes.
1981: A move to cut spending for the Departments of Labor, Health and Human Services, and Education.
1982: A move that would have forced removal of a resolution of $5.4 billion for a new jobs program.
1983: Raising Social Security retirement age to sixty-seven.
1983: An amendment adding $954.4 million for education, job training, and other social programs.
1983: A plan allowing the Federal Communications Commission to begin new charges to residential and small-business telephone users for long-distance access service.
1984: An immigration bill penalizing employers who knowingly hire illegal aliens and permitting amnesty for aliens already living in the U.S.